edited by Mel Thistle

The Mackenzie-McNaughton Wartime Letters

with introduction and epilogue
by C.J. Mackenzie

D1068935

UNIVERSITY OF TORONTO PRESS

TORONTO AND BUFFALO

© University of Toronto Press 1975
Toronto and Buffalo
Printed in Canada

ISBN 0-8020-1758-4
LC 72-185741

edited by Mel Thistle

The Mackenzie-McNaughton Wartime Letters

with introduction and epilogue
by C.J. Mackenzie

UNIVERSITY OF TORONTO PRESS

TORONTO AND BUFFALO

© University of Toronto Press 1975
Toronto and Buffalo
Printed in Canada

ISBN 0-8020-1758-4
LC 72-185741

Acknowledgments

Like all books, this one is deeply indebted to a number of people who aided in its production, outstanding among them being Susan Kent, who edited it, and Ian Montagnes, General Editor of the University of Toronto Press. Their professional work and friendly advice were invaluable. Gloria Dumoulin and Helen Cuccaro did most of the typing – and retyping. The heirs of General McNaughton gave permission for the reproduction of certain letters, and Ryerson Press gave permission to quote a passage from the published biography by John Swettenham of the General. But the main acknowledgment must go to the National Research Council of Canada, for its generous encouragement, support, and the use of its excellent facilities, particularly its Public Information Branch: Loris Racine and Alex Maton gave us the most practical kinds of aid and support, for which we are very grateful.

C.J. Mackenzie
Mel Thistle

Contents

Foreword

In World War II, the manner in which science served Canada largely depended on the apparently fortuitous coming together of three elements: General A.G.L. McNaughton, Dr C.J. Mackenzie, and the National Research Council of Canada. The most important element was the NRC. It happened to constitute exactly what was needed at the time: an organization that was *not* narrowly mission-oriented, that is, not a government department. It was a flexible institution that could be readily turned in any desired direction, and full of eager, well-trained, and able young people.

When the NRC began, in 1916, its mandate included the responsibility for co-ordinating scientific and industrial research in Canada. However, what the members of that first Advisory Council found, in their first few months of office, was that there was nothing to co-ordinate. There were not fifty full-time researchers in the physical sciences in the whole of Canada. Under these circumstances, the members of the council knew what had to be done: breed researchers. They immediately set about doing this, by awarding scholarships to graduate students in Canadian universities, and by giving grants in aid of research to professors.

Canadian industries at that time, through no fault of their own but simply as a result of natural historical processes, were lagging about a generation behind their counterparts in Great Britain and the USA in scientific sophistication. Very little industrial research was being done, at any level. Most Canadian companies considered such activity too expensive, or too long-drawn-out before economic pay-off, to undertake on their own account. The NRC therefore considered that it should establish central laboratories of its own, to provide the basis of long-term applied research on which industrial innovation must be founded.

The council had not lost sight of the program to breed researchers, or of the need to build up science in the universities. But it felt that one of its principal functions was first to do necessary things that otherwise would not be done – to plug the gaps, to create new institutions when they were needed – within the broad context of scientific support for industry. The need to establish central, long-range applied-research laboratories thus became an additional responsibility. The council had not, however, reckoned on the difficulty of persuading the government that this should be so. The new Advisory Council found that its advice to government was not always followed with notable alacrity when large sums of money were involved.

After long travail and many disappointments, the NRC laboratories were eventually established. The doors opened in 1932 – right in the middle of a great depression. The economic climate enabled Dr H.M. Tory, with the aid of his three laboratory directors, to select and employ for very little money a staff made up of the most brilliant products of the council's own scholarship and granting programs. Tory made his little money count heavily for the future in which he so profoundly believed.

By 1939, the National Research Laboratories consisted of the original divisions devoted to chemistry, biology, and physics, plus a fourth division of mechanical engineering founded in 1936 and much more heavily weighted towards applied research than its parent, the Division of Physics and Engineering. These four divisions were led by virtually autonomous directors, free to make the organizational structure follow and fit the work rather than the other way about. The president under whom these directors operated was also the chairman of the governing body, now called the National Research Council, a group of knowledgeable outside experts who normally served a maximum term of six years, consisting of two three-year appointments. Knowing that any institution free to study both basic and applied science will, in the absence of external restraints, inevitably drift towards the basic studies, the governing body kept (and still keeps) a sharp eye on the balance between basic and applied research, altering this balance from time to time to meet the changing needs of a changing society.

Unfortunately, the distinction inherent in this organizational structure is often unrecognized. Even a divisional scientist or engineer, asked where he works, is apt to reply, 'At the National Research Council' – to the continuing confusion of the public, and much of the technological community, who do not thus distinguish between the National Research *Laboratories*, where the work is done, and the National Research *Council*, a body of outside experts drawn from industries, universities, and labour. It is, after all, much easier to call the entire organization 'the NRC.' We all do it. But it tends to hide the controlling forces of the council, and the great benefits that flow from easy access to outside advisers who know what the work is about and the kinds of people needed for it, and who are free to look down the road ahead. The council in this sense is a long-range planning committee. Through it, the whole organization is able to respond swiftly and easily to changing needs.

In this task the council is helped immeasurably by its associate committees. These are replications of itself, groups of interested people who know what they are talking about and who serve without pay for a limited term, each committee consisting of key figures from industry, universities, and governments, each committee being formed (and eventually disbanded) for each specific need as it becomes apparent. This achievement is widely admired. Members serve not from altruistic motives, but because they are thereby a part of the most important developments in their own fields of interest, and are honoured to be asked to serve.

By 1939, there had evolved a supple and flexible scientific institution, capable of dealing resourcefully with any circumstance that history might offer. This capability was now to be put to the test. How was Canada to conduct, adapt, and expand a civilian scientific institution to meet the demands of world war?

So great a change was necessary that the element of 'future-shock' had to be faced a generation before the term came into common use. The past also had to be overcome. Canada had a small reputation for research, not much reputation for development, and even less reputation for sophisticated manufacturing. British scientists and statesmen, unaware of recent developments, felt that the Dominion was incapable of advanced research and therefore incapable of meticulous manufacture of, for instance, radio parts. They had to be convinced.

This brings us back to the two key figures, McNaughton and Mackenzie. They were in many ways alike. They knew each other well, in part because in a country that was still small they had graduated in engineering within a year of each other. Both also were veterans of World War I and therefore acceptable to the next generation of warriors. Not only did both understand things technical in considerable depth; they also understood people with great clarity and insight. Both had the gift of empathy, the main ingredient of the charisma of leadership. They derived vigour from belief in natural law – that what one did in the present would determine the shape of the future – and that this held true for both things and people. They shared high standards and ideals of service. But in other respects they were, of course, quite different from one another.

Andrew George Latta McNaughton, 1887–1966, lived a life of passionately devoted service to his country, documented in a three-volume biography by John Swettenham.[1] He played a number of citizen-roles, the best known being those of soldier, scientist, diplomat, and statesman. Ironically, the label most firmly attached is the first – he will always be known as *General* McNaughton – but those who knew him intimately say that, if World War I had not broken out when it did, McNaughton would never have been a soldier. He was primarily a scientist-engineer, and well up among the greatest of his time and breed.[2]

McNaughton received his Bachelor's degree in electrical engineering, with honours, from McGill University in 1910, and his Master's degree in 1912. His talents lay mainly in the practical applications of science, and he remained at McGill until war broke out in 1914, following his primary interests in electrical engineering and in the theory and practice of artillery. He published six research papers before the war interrupted what was certain to be a distinguished professional career.

McNaughton rose to command the heavy artillery of the Canadian Corps. His main interests throughout were to apply scientific methods to military problems and, above all else, to win battles with the minimum loss of life. He regarded the latter as the supreme test of the former. By war's end, he was commended by General Sir Arthur Currie as 'the best artillery officer in the British Empire.'

He was not yet, however, a member of the permanent army, and in 1918 planned to return to civilian life; he hoped to teach electrical engineering, and wrote to all Canadian university presidents, looking for a job on the faculty. But General Currie persuaded him to undertake 'temporary' duties related to demobilization and other post-war organizational problems of the armed forces. His success in these concerns led naturally to a career in the permanent force and rapid promotion to chief of the General Staff in 1929.

In 1924, the Royal Canadian Air Force came into being, and McNaughton became involved in that exciting and innovative endeavour. At that time, military budgets were being cut, yet young pilots had to be trained. McNaughton perceived that the new service should meet both military and civilian needs, and he therefore looked for funds in civil budgets. This turned his attention to the North, and he became interested in the two main problems of that vast land, transport and communication. As a result he encouraged much of the subsequent development of bush aircraft and the training of bush pilots – fields in which Canada still leads the world. Stemming out of these same interests came the cathode-ray direction finder, one of the forerunners of radar, patented by McNaughton and Major W.A. Steel (of the Royal Canadian Corps of Signals) in 1925.

McNaughton became keenly interested in the work of the National Research Council long before he was made president of that institution. He instigated the formation of a number of associate committees and served on several as chairman, including those in surveying, radio, and aerial navigation. He also influenced the council's decisions to initiate projects in fields such as ballistics.

In 1935, McNaughton was appointed president of NRC and proceeded to prepare the council's laboratories for the war that he so clearly foresaw. In 1938, during the 'peace-in-our-time' period, he strode into NRC's purchasing office and asked, courteously but firmly, that the purchasing officer 'get those microscopes that we ordered out of Austria before war is declared.' When the General had left, the PO looked around helplessly and murmured: 'What war?'

By 1939, the NRC seems to have been somewhat more ready for war than most Canadian civilian institutions. Its aerodynamic facilities were in existence for both civilian and military use. Its research in ballistics, particularly electronic methods of measuring muzzle velocities, had been under way since 1932. Work on gas masks had begun in 1937 and work on radar in 1939. Therefore war, when it came, was not altogether a stranger.

In October 1939, General McNaughton was appointed Inspector-General of Units of the First Canadian Division, and the question of his NRC successor arose. Bluntly, he asked Mackenzie King: 'When the war is over, do you want me to go back to the NRC?' Mackenzie King said that he did. McNaughton then pointed out that the Research Council Act gave the council authority to appoint an acting president during a president's absence from the country, on duty.

At this point, it seems appropriate to quote from volume two of the McNaughton biography by John Swettenham:

'I recall that he [Mackenzie King] looked at me very hard and he said: "Well, whom do you want to appoint?" ... '
McNaughton ... had his answer ready.

'Jack Mackenzie,' he replied.

The Prime Minister was aghast. 'But he's another Conservative!' he exclaimed.

'Does that really matter?' McNaughton fired back.

There was a lengthy pause during which King looked quizzically at the General.

'No, it does not,' he finally said.

As in McNaughton's case, the calibre of the man had prevailed over his personal politics. The name of Dean Mackenzie went before the council and was unanimously approved. On October 18 he arrived in Ottawa and assumed the office of acting president of NRC.[3]

McNaughton was greatly pleased with this appointment – and not merely because it was useful to the Canadian war effort and to him personally (he now had a direct channel for his own proposals to an individual who would press them forward). He considered Jack Mackenzie to be the best-qualified member of the NRC to lead the council and give continuity to the work in hand for all purposes. 'And so,' said McNaughton, 'with great initiative and distinction, he proved to be.'

Chalmers Jack Mackenzie, the new head of NRC, had been born in 1888 at St Stephen, New Brunswick, and graduated in engineering from Dalhousie University in 1909. He was notably people-oriented rather than book-oriented – most of his personal library was biographical. He played music, but in a band; his sports were contact sports; when he entered business it was in a partnership; he enjoyed dancing because it was with a partner. The part of nature that interested him was human nature: he shot ducks, he smoked, he drank – for companionship. He was interested in human communication, in the relations between words and things, and had fun with contract law and specifications because these words *had* to carry *little* detail – not much – in a universe that changes. He loved the phrase: 'finish in a *fitting* manner.'

Mackenzie had no prospect of a permanent job in the Maritimes and left in January of 1910 for western Canada. He and a classmate (Jack F. Cahan) opened an office in Saskatoon under the name of Mackenzie and Cahan, and for some months did minor surveying and inspection jobs. Then Cahan took an inspector's job and Mackenzie went to work for Mart Maxwell on the design and construction of an electric power plant in Camrose, Alberta. Maxwell, some twenty years older, was also born in St Stephen, and had practised engineering in New York till 1910. Their association led to a full partnership in the firm of Maxwell and Mackenzie. From 1910 to 1914, Mackenzie personally designed and contracted for the construction of a series of electric power plants, water and sewer installations in Alberta, from Medicine Hat to Edson, with his own head office in Edmonton.

During those four years, Mackenzie was thrown into a pioneering, booming western environment where youth, optimism, and easy money were the values of the day. He never worked under the supervision of any individual during that period (nor in any period except as a junior officer in wartime). That experience gave him a matured confidence in the handling of men and affairs that stayed with him for the rest of his life.

In October 1912, while reporting on a pipeline for distributing natural gas in Tofield, Mackenzie received a telegram from the president of the University of Saskatchewan, offering him a job for the winter. Until then, he had never considered teaching as a career. At Saskatoon, six young students wanted to register in an engineering course. Mackenzie organized and taught first-year engineering courses for 1912–13, then returned to his engineering practice in Edmonton, with no intent to continue teaching. However, he received another letter from the president asking him to return – a young engineer named C.D. Howe had offered the university a fee to test the cement for a grain elevator in Saskatoon. Thus began Mackenzie's interest in cement.

In 1913–14, Mackenzie taught all the engineering courses of the first and second years and drafted a detailed curriculum for a four-year course in civil engineering. Then he realized that he needed a graduate degree. He entered Harvard in June of 1914 and was able to obtain his MCE in twelve months (about half the normal time). Thus, that fortuitous 'job for the winter' in 1912 led him to graduate study to improve his qualifications as a scientific engineer and also as a professor and a manager of mission-oriented research.

After graduation, he enlisted in the Western University Infantry Battalion. He carried the university work for the fall term of 1915 while his substitute, J.P. Oliver, took the course in Winnipeg to qualify for a commission. Then Oliver returned to teaching while Mackenzie attended the officer-training course. At the spring convocation in 1916, students who had entered the course in 1912 got their degrees. Since all the graduates and all the staff were going overseas, the Saskatchewan Engineering School closed for the duration.

Mackenzie was in Mons on Armistice Day, got immediate leave to London and, by getting temporarily attached to Khaki University, wangled his return to Canada in January of 1919. He was awarded the Military Cross in 1918.

While there is little else about it to recommend trench warfare, Mackenzie did come out of World War I with a firm resolution that, in future, he would allow nothing in the way of misfortunes, violent confrontations, or frustrations to upset him in any emotional way. Keeping this resolution made for his efficiency, objectivity, and peace of mind under those conditions of temporary confusion that lay ahead.

Relief from the war gave him an enormous zest and energy to get busy at something real and useful. Until the Engineering School reopened in September, Mackenzie was busy as chairman of the committee of the Engineering Institute of Canada on the deterioration of concrete exposed to alkali ground waters. He soon realized that the normal ad hoc solutions, such as adding compounds to cement mixtures and protecting surfaces of exposed structures, would never solve the difficulties. What was needed was an attack by a team of pure researchers into the chemical reactions involved.

Mackenzie persuaded his colleague, Dr Thorbergur Thorvaldson, professor of chemistry at the University of Saskatchewan, to take leave of absence to recruit and direct a small staff, plus his graduate students, for this project. Mackenzie raised the money from industries, governments, railways; and eventually the NRC took over the full costs of this distinguished research, which continued for several years after the practical problem had disappeared. Many papers were published and, in 1927, the Plummer Medal of the EIC was awarded to Thorvaldson and Mackenzie for one of these papers.

Getting involved in the alkali-research work not only gave Mackenzie a great immediate lift but also something else of more importance to his future: the realization of the importance of involving both pure and applied scientists in difficult, mission-oriented problems; and that such co-operation leads to efficiency, mutual respect, and understanding.

Mackenzie became dean of Engineering in 1921. The Engineering School grew rapidly, from ten students registered in 1921, to two hundred in 1931 and five hundred in 1941. The school achieved status as one of the better ones in Canada and its degrees were accepted in graduate schools in the USA and in the UK. The staff received many honours.

In the 1920s Mackenzie's interest in town planning arose out of his previous work on designing water-distribution systems, in which estimating future population growth of towns and cities was a primary factor in rational design. In 1929, he published a well-received study of the probable growth of Saskatoon. He pointed out that, because of the extravagant propaganda of real-estate agents in the fantastic boom days, land in

Saskatoon (with a population of about 25,000) had been subdivided and sold in quantities sufficient to serve a city of about half a million population. One serious aspect was that zoning by-laws had estimated the required business areas in a similarly optimistic way. He estimated that the population of Saskatoon, in 1955, would amount to 96,000. (Actually, in the census of 1961, it was 95,526 – and if the six war years are subtracted, this is bang on.) This study persuaded Mackenzie to accept the chairmanship of the city planning board in 1928.

The board engaged A.E.K. Bunnell, an experienced and able town planner. His final report proposed a reduction in areas zoned for business, the prohibiting of building houses on twenty-five-foot lots, and the retrieval of a significant section of downtown commercial property which was steadily degenerating into a slum. To retrieve this area, he suggested a bridge over the river at Broadway Street as the only cure. Mackenzie became keen about the over-all proposals and addressed, on request, many public groups. The mayor of Saskatoon, a friend of Mackenzie, said to him: 'I will support the project but if you really want quick action you must run for a seat on council – the formal publishing of reports from royal commissioners and other bodies seldom results in action until someone associated with the study becomes a part of the "seat of power." '

Mackenzie followed this advice, was elected to the city council and, during his year of office (1928–9), got the plans accepted and the necessary by-laws passed. When the report came out, Mackenzie encouraged a fourth-year student (Bev Evans) to take as his thesis a design study for a bridge as recommended by Bunnell. No one thought that such a structure would be built for many years. But a fortuitous sequence of events occurred. A deep depression struck; relief measures were hastily instituted; a bridge in Saskatoon was accepted by the federal government as a suitable relief project – and the seemingly isolated studies permitted the building of this bridge in the unbelievably short over-all time of twelve months.

In his summer holiday periods, from 1921 to 1939, Mackenzie was retained by practising engineers as a consultant on many small projects. His major outside professional jobs, for which he took leave of absence from the university, were the design and construction supervision of two sizable concrete bridges, the Broadway Bridge over the South Saskatchewan River in Saskatoon, and the Borden Bridge over the North Saskatchewan River at the Ceepee Crossing near Battleford.

The Broadway Bridge was thirteen hundred feet including approaches and spanned a river about one thousand feet wide. The total cost was less than a million dollars. Mackenzie's total engineering staff consisted of four of his students who had graduated the year before. The already available design made it possible to let a construction contract one month after the project was authorized. Work started on 12 December 1931, and it was opened for traffic the following November 11.

All labour had to be requisitioned from the local relief office; no machinery could be used for work that could be done by hand, and most of the labourers could be allowed to work for only one week. During the year, 1,593 different men were employed. Regulations were strict: a man with no children could not earn more than $25 per month, while the maximum for a man with a large family was $37.50.

The piers had to be completed before the high-water spring floods. This meant eighteen-hour working days for the four designing engineers, to have working plans ready for the next morning. This continued until the bridge was opened.

While Mackenzie was on city council he was appointed to the board of governors of the Saskatoon City Hospital. He served as chairman of the board in 1937-9. This was not a cushy job; it involved financial, professional, and sensitive human affairs, and a civilian chairman had to develop the art of diplomacy to survive. This experience helped him to respect doctors and better understand the problems of medical administration and research, and made for the later, pleasant co-operation with doctors administering the medical-research committees of the NRC.

He became a member of the Honorary Advisory Council of the NRC in 1935, and was soon vigorously at work as chairman of its Review Committee. Their job was to look down the road ahead, and to recommend suitable changes to enable the NRC to serve the actual needs of the country as they surfaced and became apparent. He became acting president of the NRC in 1939.

With huge territory and a relatively sparse population (per square mile, about enough for a game of bridge), Canada has long perforce been deeply interested in transport and communication. These concerns have led to both the largest and the second-largest railway systems on earth and to the longest television system, running through seven time zones and two cultures. It was in Canada that photogrammetry was born. Nor has software been neglected: the quality of content of French-Canadian television is the envy of France, and the two present world leaders in the discipline of 'general semantics,' S.I. Hayakawa and Samuel Bois, were both born in Canada. The human side of communication has a long and distinguished history in this country, notably in Quebec, western Canada and, later, in Ontario.

In World War II, as a counterpoint to its associate-committee activity, the National Research Council of Canada gave particular attention to both formal and informal communication with opposite numbers in Britain and the USA, as well as among the experts within Canada. Exhaustive use was made of such visiting bodies as the Tizard mission. Some council scientists transferred themselves bodily into new industries, founded on their own labours; others served in the front lines in all theatres of war, testing their devices. Always, the greatest importance was given to firm (but tactful) transfer of vital information the moment it became available in useful form. Something of this sort seems to happen in all wars everywhere, but Canada happened to be naturally concerned with good communication and consciously exploited the possibilities engendered by wartime urgency and devotion.

An excellent example of highly efficient, warm, human communication, achieved in times of stress, emerges in the remarkable series of letters that constitutes the bulk of this book. By what now appears as a happy administrative accident, Dr Mackenzie was acting president of NRC for the first three years of the war while General McNaughton, the president, was on leave of absence as commander of Canada's field forces. Mackenzie wrote a secret letter to the general every six weeks or so, reporting on the more important developments under way in the council's laboratories.

By the end of 1943, the period for novel scientific discovery and development was over. Thereafter, the major emphasis was on industrial production and field operations. But the early years were more exciting and stimulating – full of venture – and this is the period covered by these letters.

As previously noted, the operation of large civilian, scientific institutions during a war was new to Canada; Dr Mackenzie became the first Canadian conductor to wield the baton in such an enterprise. His letters give us an unusual opportunity to observe how the council evolved under the pressure of war (and, in the epilogue, the quality of forethought concerning its future development when peace should come again). They show how the NRC was turned from a peace-time operation into a war machine, and enlarged from a body of three hundred persons to an institution of thirteen hundred smoothly operating full-time personnel (and many hundreds more in the advisory structure), without faltering or missing a step. Through the forty-three associate committees and their

seventy-three subcommittees, every relevant Canadian scientific establishment and laboratory in government, industry and university, was
welded into a single, smoothly functioning implement of war.

In the letters that follow, we can see one highly placed engineer
communicating with another about Canada's part in the most important
venture in the world at the time, and in the common tongue, easily
grasped by an intelligent layman. It is fortunate for Canadian history that
these two men had an ocean between them, an ability to speak forthrightly
together, and the acting-president arrangement; otherwise, these letters
would never have been written.

Their writing has an elegance all its own: a strong, clean, workmanlike
structure without an ounce of superfluous material anywhere. Neither
man thought of himself as an author in the literary sense; but it was
characteristic of them, in their natural courtesy, to build an elegant
structure – in words just as in other media. It never occurred to them that
these letters, written as best they could be in the press of war, responding
to urgencies of the moment, might one day be published for a later
generation. They simply wrote as they thought, and the result is first-class
science reporting: crisp, clear, straightforward, free of triviality.

In a war, all resources must be concentrated on 'certainties,' as nearly
as possible. But the future cannot be fully known; some failures are
inevitable. Some council war activities failed to pay off: chief among these
was the grandiose proposal for floating airports, made out of ice, coded
'Habakkuk,' which turned out to be impractical.[4] The work on wooden
aircraft also failed to get off the ground. The brilliant work on camouflage
was rendered obsolete by the equally brilliant work on radar. Others of
the council's successful programs were so secret that they are barely (and
obscurely) mentioned in one or two of these 'secret' letters. Chief among
these is the NRC atomic-energy project – a story that has since been told.[5]

The prime essential of new enterprise is always courage. For a military
commander, such as McNaughton, this need is obvious. For the commander of scientific enterprises, such as Mackenzie, the point may be a little
more subtle; but those who consider the welfare of a state must be vividly
aware of it – for example, Nicolo Machiavelli, who noted in *The Prince*
that:

There is nothing more difficult to take in hand, more perilous to conduct, or more
uncertain in its success, than to take the lead in the introduction of a new order of
things.

This saying applied in full force to Mackenzie, whose lot it was, more than that of any other man, to usher Canada into her atomic age. Machiavelli noted the difficulty involved; but he also noted, twenty chapters later, that, 'Where the willingness is great, the difficulties cannot be great.' And, in fact, that is how Mackenzie did it.

Most of the council's rigorous choices of what to do in the war, and how to go about it, did in fact pay off. These programs included uses of radar for land, sea, and air, the first Canadian optical-glass industry, the new process for producing metallic magnesium (ending dependence on imports), the pressure suit and other advances in aviation medicine, degaussing and other defences against ingenious varieties of destructive German mines, the work on inspection of munitions in the council's gauge laboratory, temporary refrigeration of ships' holds for carrying bacon to Britain, the defensive work on war gases, and work on ballistics.

Dr C.J. Mackenzie was the man at the centre. He was like a great spider in the middle of an enormous web. His letters form a fascinating insight, not only into NRC and Canadian science at war, but into the whole workings of science with government and industry. By wise use of the council's flexible structure, of the associate-committee network, of his service (usually as chairman) on some twenty other national boards and committees in closely related fields, and of his own outstanding qualities, he gathered, focused, and led every possibly useful member of Canada's entire scientific community. Not least among the many qualities that enabled him to attain these objectives was his skill as a communicator. Exactly how he went about it is revealed in the wartime letters.

The most valuable by-product of adequate face-to-face communication between the right people at the right time is the respect developed on both sides. The council ended the war holding respect for and being respected by the key ministers of the Crown and the top people in the armed services, government departments, industries, and universities of Canada, and a goodly number of key figures in other countries.

The epilogue is an important part of this book. It yields the same authentic flavour as that of the letters themselves, because it is based on the personal journals kept daily by Mackenzie, and covers the period from the last of the letters in 1943 to the end of his presidency of Atomic Energy of Canada Limited in 1953. If anything, his achievements during this decade were even more important for the growth of science in Canada than those related in the letters.

Mackenzie at that time had two things going for him: his impressive skills as a communicator, now sharp and keen from practice and the steels of war; and that vital need, a listener in high places. C.D. Howe was apparently the first member of any Canadian cabinet who was able to listen effectively to the voice of science. As Lord Hailsham said in 1963: 'It is not enough to buy a scientific mind. You must have it yourself if you wish to use it in others.' Or, as E.W.R. Steacie remarked, some years earlier, what is the use of throwing a ball if there is no catcher anywhere in sight?

Without the team of Mackenzie and Howe, with their mutual high regard and the amity of work well done together, the impressive scientific complex built up by Canada during the war – greater by an order of magnitude in 1945 than it had been in 1939 – would probably have been largely disbanded following the ancient practices of a nation newly come to peace, when mighty efforts are relaxed because the more obvious needs have disappeared. This was the generally anticipated pattern. But Mackenzie was convinced that the scientific world was entering an entirely new era in its history, a period of explosive growth. He foresaw a technological revolution. He was able to convince C.D. Howe that this was so and, through Howe, to sway the cabinet. So, in the end, Mackenzie kept what he had won, with promise of increasingly massive support. Therefore, in the last two years of the war, those who cared about the future of science in Canada had the happy task of reconversion, rather than demobilization.

Could the NRC itself easily reconvert to peace? And on the new and much higher level required by Mackenzie's vision of the future? Early in the war, the NRC had transferred its energies to war problems with such success that it soon became the research branch for the Department of Munitions and Supply, and for all three armed services. By the end of 1943, it had the support of governments, the confidence of the armed services, the good will of industries, the sympathy of universities. This happy situation made another rapid transformation possible, and, by 1945, the basic reconversion of the NRC was reasonably complete.

Mackenzie's forward thinking continued to exhibit itself in action. In 1947, the NRC was able to free itself from most of the war work with the establishment of the Defence Research Board.[6] Within its own laboratory structure, the council established a Division of Building Research, closely linked and integrated with the industry it served, and a Radio and Electrical Engineering Division. The Prairie Regional Laboratory was established in 1948, and the Atlantic Regional Laboratory in 1952. The Division of Applied Chemistry was also opened in 1952 and the Division of Applied Physics in 1955. In 1959, the aeronautical laboratories became the National Aeronautical Establishment, near the Uplands airport; and in 1960 the medical-research committees became the Medical Research Council.

These new scientific institutions, evolving from the fabric of the NRC, had been foreshadowed by Mackenzie in 1944, as noted in the epilogue. He had the great pleasure of assisting with five of these live births while he was president of the National Research Council from 1944 to 1952.

The council's atomic-energy project, begun in 1942, gave rise to Atomic Energy of Canada Limited in 1952. In that year Dr Mackenzie resigned as head of the NRC to become the first president of Atomic Energy of Canada Limited, and to pilot the new organization through its first year of operations.

Where past and future intersect, in the glowing moment of the now, some things need to be said again and again. In his letters and in his epilogue, Mackenzie was concerned with timely production of physical artifacts and with efficient processes and services. He was concerned with the birth, growth, and welfare of science-based institutions that would match the growing needs of his country. He was vitally concerned with quality, as well as with quantity. All these concerns were part of his mandate, and all were brilliantly accomplished. A number of our modern, science-based institutions were built first in the mind of C.J. Mackenzie, some of them after he had officially retired.

Yet he never turned his mind away from the higher qualities of human communication; from warmth, friendliness, deep understanding, and high regard for the better aspects of all those with whom he had to deal; from the firm conviction that, in the end, it is the people who count, that it is humans who matter in the flow of time. There was iron in him; but he was no sun dial, marking only the sunny hours. He was quick to apprehend the faults and flaws that pepper all who are human. He did not suffer fools gladly; but he knew where the balance lay, and what should be encouraged, what denied. Like McNaughton before him and like Steacie, who came after, he knew when to exert the catalytic powers of trust and belief. Great teacher to the end of his formal service, and after, he brought out the best in all of us. This book constitutes one thin slice through his life and work, but it holds enough savour to reveal his quality, and a set of deeds and attitudes with power to endure.

1 John Swettenham, *McNaughton* (Toronto: Ryerson Press, 1968)
2 See the biography by C.J. Mackenzie in the *Proceedings of the Royal Society of Canada* (1967), pp. 91–106

3 Swettenham, *McNaughton*, pp. 5, 6
4 Wilfred Eggleston, *Scientists at War* (Toronto and London: Oxford University
   Press, 1950), pp. 153–9
5 See Wilfred Eggleston, *Canada's Nuclear Story* (Toronto: Clarke Irwin, 1965)
6 See D.J. Goodspeed, *DRB: A History of the Defence Research Board of Canada*
   (Ottawa: Queen's Printer, 1958)

THE MACKENZIE-MCNAUGHTON
WARTIME LETTERS

C.J. MACKENZIE

Introduction

In the months immediately preceding World War II most knowledgeable people were certain that war was inevitable and that Canada would become involved in some way. During these months there was much academic debate as to whether Canada would automatically follow Great Britain into a war for which she was neither enthusiastic nor militarily prepared. True, in 1937 Prime Minister Mackenzie King, in spite of strong opposition from his own party, had increased defence expenditures sharply and, in 1938, he had noted in his diary that 'if war broke out and Canadian freedom was threatened I would recommend participation.' In 1939, after Hitler annexed Bohemia and Moravia, the PM stated in Parliament that, 'in certain circumstances, the Government would recommend action by Canada to resist aggression.'[1] When war did break out, the immediate positive action was equally cautious.

When Great Britain declared war on September 3, 1939, strong pressure was put on the government by groups in Canada to follow Britain's example immediately: surprisingly, much of this pressure came from those who formerly had been denouncing wars. On the other hand, powerful pressure came from responsible officials in Britain and the United States[2] to delay a declaration of war as long as possible, to permit the delivery to neutral Canada of war supplies from the United States which could not legally be shipped, by that country, to any belligerent country such as England. Consequently, the Canadian government, apparently feeling that it would be politically unwise to delay declaration of war more than one week, came in on 10 September 1939, a bit confused about the scale of operation and with no intention of immediately mounting an all-out war effort. It was generally felt that the war would be a short one and that Canada should concentrate on supply of materiel, a limited expeditionary force, an Air Force training program and an enlarged Navy. A bill establishing a Department of Munitions and Supply was passed in September 1939, but was not proclaimed until April 1940, and the Honourable C.D. Howe, who was named minister, did not give up his major portfolio, the Department of Transport, until July 5.

This so-called phoney-war period ended abruptly in mid-June 1940; France had fallen, Italy had declared war, and Great Britain stood naked and alone in Europe. The initial reaction of Canadians was shock and gloom, but this quickly turned to determination. Money no longer was master; the ultimate goal became total destruction of Hitlerian aggression at any cost: it was a new kind of war.

There never was any uncertainty about the inevitability of another major world war in the mind of General A.G.L. McNaughton, president of the National Research Council of Canada. As early as 1937, he had been sure that such a conflict could break out at any time and, characteristically, he did something about it. His experiences had convinced him that scientific research and development would play a major role in future wars and, therefore, without disturbing the normal operation of the National Research laboratories, he had encouraged certain research scientists to concentrate on specific projects, in the general area of their training and interests, which would be of real importance in case of war. The result was that by the fall of 1939, small but enthusiastic groups were working expertly on such things as radar, production of optical glass, ballistics, gauge testing, gas masks, and many other projects in aeronautics, physics, and chemistry.

When war was declared, these units went on active service at once, and soon most of the other laboratories had turned, in practice, from a civilian to a defence role. Such a quick adjustment was relatively easy because well-trained scientists, like medical staffs, are by basic training competent to deal with either military or civilian technical problems. The early start also brought quick recognition, by technical military officers, of the National Research Council as an effective wartime unit.

By the middle of August 1940, NRC research scientists had designed, built, and installed a small early-warning radar facility to protect Halifax harbour. Numerous other types of military equipment were already in prototype form, and a large, fully operational gauge-testing laboratory was servicing gauges for industrial munitions plants. In fact, the National

Research Council was on a war basis sooner than most other organizations in Canada; but it was handicapped by government regulations under which it was still designated as a non-war unit, although it had become, in reality, the research establishment of the armed services and special adviser to C.D. Howe.

In addition to the war work in NRC laboratories, several individuals and groups in government, university, and industrial laboratories had become interested in projects of their own choosing. However, the only sizable and well-organized research program in this category was Sir Frederick Banting's laboratories at the University of Toronto, which had been started in 1939. Sir Frederick, like General McNaughton, had been certain that war would come soon, and he too proceeded to do something about it. He became the central figure in organizing aviation medical research in his own laboratories in co-operation with Air Force pilots. In June 1939, at Banting's urging, the Department of National Defence, by Order in Council, set up a committee on aviation medical research and made a personal grant of sixteen thousand dollars to Banting. From the budget of his own laboratory at the University of Toronto, Banting spent thirty-five thousand dollars during the six-month period from October 1939 to March 1940. The committee was reorganized in May 1940, and became the Associate Committee of the National Research Council on Aviation Medical Research, with a budget of $109,000. This wartime associate committee was disbanded in 1945, after an outstanding record of achievement.

Sir Frederick, as chairman of the associate committee until his tragic death, used to recall with amusement an incident that occurred as the result of hastily drafted wartime regulations. When war was declared, Banting's grant from the Department of Defence for aviation medical research was immediately cancelled by the deputy minister's office on the basis that 'research was not an essential wartime activity that could be supported by the Defence Department'; needless to say, this interpretation by minor officials of the value of research was not supported by the armed forces and senior civil servants, nor did it have any effect on future research activities.

During the phoney-war period, before the council was recognized as a war unit, there were many administrative hurdles to overcome. For instance, in our supplementary war estimates for 1939–40, the item for 'contingencies,' which was a large portion of the total, was deleted because itemized details were not shown; yet contingencies were about the most realistic item submitted. Another sweeping general order came through at that time instructing us that, because the National Research Council was not a war unit, our 1940–41 estimates would have to be cut back to the 1936–7 level of expenditure. As the council laboratories had only been opened (with a skeleton staff) in 1932, such a cut would have meant stopping all our war work as a wartime economy measure. Of course, all such instructions were cancelled as soon as senior officials and ministers could be briefed. Administrative road-blocks were apparently inevitable during the early transition days of war; still, although no long-term effect resulted, such matters cost administrative staffs valuable time and energy.

Because the National Research Council was not early recognized as a war unit, our scientists were not eligible for pension protection during the early months, and never was their pension greater than that of an Army lieutenant; it was for this reason that Sir Frederick Banting went into uniform as a major when he undertook that fateful trip to England. Yet many of the council's scientific officers were exposed to serious war risks: a team of senior aeronautical engineers flew without protection for several months, searching for 'icing conditions' in order to test de-icing equipment under development; another scientist was aboard the British battleship *Rodney* when it engaged the German battleship *Bismarck* in a deadly duel of gunfire (not a particularly safe place for non-combat personnel).

There were other regulations regarding ceilings on staff increases, salaries, classifications, and promotions that caused difficulties for a while. In 1939, the council's machine shop was staffed by a small but highly expert group of instrument makers. Immediately war started, great demands came from many departments for production of special war instruments. This called for a large increase in temporary staff. Authority was obtained to hire machinists on a temporary basis and to pay them high, wartime rates of pay, but the salaries of our permanent expert staff, who had to instruct and supervise such temporary staff, were frozen at depression salaries well below current prevailing rates. Promotions and revised salaries were routine in the armed forces and other designated war units. Eventually, I requested permission to present our case directly to Treasury Board, and immediately got quick and sympathetic action. The ministers had been unaware of our difficulties, for the interpretation and implications of general regulations were dealt with by bureaucratic civil servants. I will never forget my relief when the chairman of the Treasury Board, the Honourable J.L. Ilsley, said to one of the secretaries: 'Is that the situation?' 'Yes, sir,' was the answer. 'Well that is unreasonable and intolerable. I want it changed at once.' That was the last of such road-blocks for the National Research Council.

By mid-1940, our financing was made far more flexible by generous free gifts of over one million dollars to the government by a few Canadian corporations. The only reservation made by the donors was that the money must be used for support of immediate war projects. After consideration, the government decided that this free money could best be used for wartime research, and set up a War Technical and Scientific Development Committee to administer the fund and with power to make unrestricted grants to projects recommended by the acting president of the National Research Council. This free money was used to start immediately and informally most of the projects which proved of greatest success in our war work. For instance, the fund allowed us to expand immediately the Radio Section of the NRC, which by early 1940 had already built and installed radar protection at Halifax harbour. It was a pump-priming fund, allowing the council to start work on projects long before government funds could be processed formally by Treasury, at a time when the government had not yet really accepted NRC as a wartime unit and, in fact, was not much aware of science as a useful arm of government operations.

This pump-priming process worked well. It helped us in getting a flying start on our war efforts. The government soon took over most of our financial liabilities and we had no further financial barriers during the war. Indeed, the industrial members of the fund committee were much impressed by the fact that, after financing the early start of projects involving several millions of dollars, by war's end the cash on hand in the fund exceeded the cash we had started with. Time gained in this fashion had other happy results as well, of great import: the early success in radar developments, for instance, convinced the Departments of Defence and of Munitions and Supply that the National Research Council was capable of developing, designing, and producing sophisticated and practical military equipment.

All of these incidents combined to give NRC an early, flexible wartime structure, based on informality and personal confidence, that was the envy of scientists in our allied countries.

A major problem, which caused much concern and serious thought in the early months of war, was how to mobilize for action the army of scientists and engineers from all over Canada who had offered their services to NRC as soon as war was declared. We could and did, of course, increase the size of the small teams then in operation at NRC, who were well informed about their detailed on-going projects, but we knew nothing of the over-all strategic and tactical scientific needs of a modern war, nor did we have, at that time, official contacts with any of the scientific, military, and political leaders who were formulating plans in Britain. Most of the scientists and engineers who had volunteered were eager to become involved immediately. Nevertheless, I was determined that we should not encourage or permit these able people to start work on problems of uncertain validity, for it would be demoralizing to have patriotic researchers work their hearts out only to find later, even if their efforts proved successful, that the devices they had developed were either already in use, or had been discarded as of no practical value in war. The other horn of the dilemma was the possible danger of frustrating young people who wanted to get into action at once and who might become disillusioned and bitter over what they would probably call bureaucratic and fumbling delays in 'getting along with the war.'

Fortunately, three events occurred in the middle months of 1940, which combined to solve this dilemma and lay the basis for the success of the National Research Council in the five years of war ahead. These events were the visit in May 1940 of Professor A.V. Hill to the Research Council; the arrival in July of Professor R.H. Fowler, who became liaison officer to the NRC; and the first visit to Ottawa, in early August, of Sir Henry Tizard.

Professor A.V. Hill was scientific adviser to the United Kingdom ambassador to Washington. His visit to Ottawa in May 1940 started NRC liaison with British scientists and war establishments. Hill was not only a distinguished scientist, Nobel laureate, and member of Parliament representing Cambridge University, but also a most understanding human. I told him of my concern that we employ our able young Canadian scientists in the most effective way and insisted that, if Canadian scientists were to be of maximum usefulness, we must have immediately a liaison officer knowledgeable about war plans in England and an authority in his own right. Hill saw the point immediately. He said that he was going back to England in a few days, and would see that our request was met. His standing in England helped to persuade a Cambridge professor, R.H. (later Sir Ralph) Fowler, a distinguished mathematical physicist, an ex-artillery officer in World War I, and, at the time, a member of most of the secret scientific war committees in Britain, to come to Canada for a year. Fowler arrived in July 1940, and the advice and information he gave us during the year he was here were of immeasurable help in selecting and planning projects of real importance.

Within a month of Fowler's coming, the Tizard mission arrived on this continent, charged with the task of disclosing to the American services the British experience with scientific weaponry under actual battle conditions. Three Canadians joined the mission in Washington and quickly became completely informed about what was happening and the needs in all fields of military operations. In addition, the members of the mission became and remained our personal friends. Professor (later Sir John) Cockcroft, who was to play a major role in our joint project in atomic energy, came to Canada and spent many hours giving our radar-research group the benefit of his recent experience in that field. Colonel F.C. (later Brigadier) Wallace, an Army representative on the mission, also came to Ottawa on a visit, but remained (as a seconded British officer attached to NRC) for the duration of the war. He played an indispensable role in producing practical radar equipment at National Research Council and Research Enterprises Limited.

Combined with McNaughton's foresight, the early help of high-ranking British liaison officers and the Tizard mission gave Canada a head start of at least two or three years on real war problems and, of more importance, an even greater head start in developing a sound base for post-war scientific and industrial technology.

The Mackenzie-McNaughton letters were not planned; they just happened. They were personal, and never thought of as official in any way. The General and I had been colleagues and personal friends from 1935 to 1939: he was president of the National Research Council and I was a member of the Honourary Council. We worked closely on council business and, when he was recalled to active service, it was he who recommended that I should become acting president during his absence on military duty.

When the official change in office occurred, it was done in typical military fashion. He had requested me to come to his office at noon on 18 October 1939, and when I was ushered in, at the exact minute, the General stood up, handed me the keys to his office, and said: 'I am going into uniform this afternoon; the command is now yours. We will now go to lunch.' We did go to lunch, but food was incidental. He took me to the Rideau Club as the most likely place to meet senior people involved in urgent war business. He introduced me to many of his acquaintances, not just as his successor, but as a personal friend. Introductions from one who enjoyed such a high standing both as a soldier and as a scientist opened many doors and avenues for immediate personal contacts, so essential for expediting rapid adjustments of the day.

I saw the General several times before he went overseas, but he never offered any specific advice or instructions as to how the National Research Council should adjust to its new role: he did not believe in dual command.

He always made formal appointments when he visited me to enquire whether the council's laboratories could be used to further one of his defence projects.

While, characteristically, General McNaughton's undivided attention was focused firmly on his immediate and primary responsibility of building an effective army, I knew he had an abiding interest in the council and thought he might be interested in hearing, from time to time, what was happening to that organization while he was in England. His early response to my first letters showed such an interest and our correspondence continued to flow naturally over four years until the end of 1943, when the General gave up his command in England.

The letters covered a particularly significant period in the history of the National Research Council, when Canadian science and technology was maturing rapidly under the stress and strains of war. This was a most stimulating period for original and imaginative ideas, innovation, production of novel prototypes in laboratories, and their adaptation to mass-production procedures in industrial factories. The letters leave off at the end of 1943, when invasion plans were in the final stages, the rate of industrial production of war supplies had reached its peak, and the demands on the National Research Council were turning to technical support for industry and assistance in developing procedures for tactical use of sophisticated equipment in combat.

As has been said, the letters were not part of a planned program; mine were spontaneous, dictated hastily, in moments borrowed from busy days, and never revised. The introduction and epilogue were first drafted in 1970 but are based on facts and opinions noted in my personal journals of 1940–53, and in numerous speeches, memoranda, taped recordings, and informal discussions with scientific officers who held key positions during the war years. The letters are arranged, not in strict chronological order, but in the order in which they were actually sent and received by my office.

1 J.W. Pickersgill, ed., *The Mackenzie King Record*, vol. 1, *1939–44* (Toronto: University of Toronto Press, 1960)

2 *Ibid.*, p. 31

The Letters

Aldershot Camp, Hampshire
31 December 1939

Dear Dean Mackenzie:

My wife has given me your letter to her of 14 December 1939, and I wish
to take this first opportunity of saying to you and through you to the
members of the National Research Council how very deeply I appreciate
the resolution which was placed on record at the 128th meeting.

The period of my association with the council has been to me, one of
the happiest and most pleasant experiences of my life, and I thoroughly
enjoyed my contacts with the members of the staff and with our many
associates and committees in the universities and in industry. My only
regret is that it had to come to an end, at least for a time, as there are many
things to be done in which I would have liked to have had a hand.
However, as I said personally to you before I left Ottawa, I am content
that the direction of affairs has passed into your hands and I feel that both
you and the council will give continuity of policy and of action in the great
projects which are under way, and that you will institute new projects
boldly as needs may indicate.

Things here are going along very well indeed. The men are splendid.
Our organization is evolving steadily to meet the rising tide of administra-
tive and training problems. There is the greatest of goodwill on all sides –
War Office, Command Headquarters, Canadian Military Headquarters,

High Commissioner's Office, etc. – and the public of Great Britain have opened their hearts and homes to us in most generous hospitality. We are getting down seriously to training and I have every hope the force will be battleworthy before long.

Please give my kindest regards to the members of the council and the staff, and with best wishes,

Very sincerely yours

A.G.L. McNAUGHTON
Major-General
GOC First Canadian Division

PS – I always use the wrist watch the council gave me and it is a constant reminder of very happy associations.

Ottawa
18 January 1940

Dear General McNaughton:

I received your letter of December 31 and was delighted to hear from you. We all feel highly complimented that in the midst of your onerous duties you find time to write a note to us. I had copies of your Christmas cable greeting sent to all the members of council and circulated it also among the members of our staff, and I assure you that the letters I received in return and the remarks made personally to me indicated real appreciation of your thoughtfulness.

I have been intending to write to you for some time and give you news of how things are going here, ... but due to pressure of work Mr [S.P.] Eagleson has not been able to get the minutes [of our last council meeting] out to date, so I will proceed without them.

The last council meeting, held on December 14, went off reasonably well, and I think there was general agreement that we were proceeding with our war activities in an effective and efficient manner. It was a busy time for me, as on the Sunday preceding the meeting a rather important matter developed in connection with the Department of Defence which took my entire time Sunday, Sunday night and Monday. On Tuesday and Wednesday we had meetings of the Review Committee and of the Assisted Researches Committee, and I had little time to prepare for the council meeting. However, as I said, I think things went off fairly well.

The matters which have been most demanding on my time are naturally those connected with the war, but I think that we have now broken the back of the organizing work. I was anxious that the handling of the special war appropriation should be done in a manner that would leave no scope for criticism, either at the present or in the future, and I think that we have now in operation a system that is sound both from the standpoint of approving projects and accounting.

I followed your suggestion of utilizing the Assisted Researches Committee, but found that when it came to considering secret projects it was impossible to disclose details to the Assisted Researches Committee, and that also a great many of the other projects had to be initiated before it was possible to call a formal meeting of the committee. It also became apparent that it was not a matter of setting aside a certain sum of money for a project, but rather one of accepting a project as being a proper one to work on, and then assuming the responsibility for the necessary financial support that would be required. Again, I was anxious that all projects which were accepted and worked upon should not be open to any criticism as to their propriety as war problems, either now or later.

Accordingly, I presented the following scheme to council: that there be set up special subcommittees of the Assisted Researches Committee on Chemistry, Physics, Biology, Mechanical Engineering, and General; that each of these committees have a chairman, who would be a member of council, and two or three other members, one of whom would be the director of the research division concerned, with power to act between meetings of the main committee. For Chemistry I suggested [Otto] Maass, [E.W.R.) Steacie, [R.K.] Stratford; for Physics, [E.F.] Burton, [R.W.] Boyle, [J.A.] Gray, and [D.A.] Keys; for Biology, Archbishop [Alexandre] Vachon, [Robert] Newton, Swaine; for Mechanical Engineering, [E.P.] Fetherstonhaugh, [J.H.] Parkin, and [D.F.] Stedman.* I had prepared project forms, a copy of which I am enclosing. The identifying letters designate the division and whether the work is being done externally or internally; for example, in the Chemistry Division, all internal problems are marked ci, and a block of numbers ranging from one hundred up is used to identify the problem within the division. External problems in chemistry are marked ce, with a corresponding block of numbers from one to one hundred. The same procedure is carried out in each division.

*A selected biographical index begins on page 153.

When any project is proposed, if it is considered suitable I first obtain the signatures of the subcommittee and, for the purposes of accounting records in the office, I approve it and a financial limit up to which expenditures may be made on the authority of the secretary's office.

For strictly secret researches, such as those carried out by [J.T.] Henderson and [E.A.] Flood,* I have arranged with Colonel [K.S.] Maclachlan, deputy minister of Defence, that he will initial the project so that we can say to our minister that it is a direct reference by the Department of National Defence. After a project has been accepted, work proceeds in the normal way, and expenditures and appointments to staff are made on the forms which have been drafted and which are OK'd by the minister.

Before each meeting of council these projects will be laid before the Assisted Researches Committee, which will confirm our action. A report will then be made to the council, and formal council approval obtained. This procedure is simple and easy to operate and places us in a strong position, as our sequence of scientific approval and authority cannot be questioned, and if anybody should raise a point in Parliament, or elsewhere, the answer is definite that we have taken the best scientific advice obtainable, that our records are in good order, and our accounting system according to government practice.

You will be interested to know that up to the present time we have under way four projects in the Biology Department; eight in the Physics Department; two in Mechanical Engineering; twelve internal projects in the Chemistry Department; and over twenty projects being undertaken by the various chemistry departments in the universities across Canada, most of which, although small and inexpensive, may ultimately prove valuable.

I expect that we will spend most of our special war grant this year, but I think that the results will be acceptable.

My relations with the Department of National Defence are good. General [W.H.P.] Elkins, of course, has been very helpful, and I have had many personal interviews with Colonel Maclachlan, who also lives at the Roxborough and whom I see informally from time to time.

Our relationships with the War Supply Board are also good. Mr [Wallace R.] Campbell has asked me lately to do several things personally which, while not in the ordinary course of duty, are an indication of confidence.

Another thing which will interest you, I feel, is the Inventions Board.

*On, respectively, radar and chemical warfare.

When it appeared that nothing was going to be done on the larger board, I worked out a scheme for an inventions board to be organized under the auspices of the Research Council. The scheme has been approved, and I am waiting now for an official Order in Council to make it authoritative. The scheme is somewhat as follows.

The board itself will consist of three members – myself as chairman, Wallace Campbell from the War Supply Board, and Colonel Maclachlan from the Department of National Defence – with S.J. Cook as secretary of the board and responsible for the work of the junior examining board. The examining committee is to consist of Ruedy, physicist, [Adrien] Cambron, chemist, and [K.F.] Tupper, engineer. The examining committee will receive all suggestions and inventions submitted, examine them as to their scientific soundness, discard the perpetual-motion schemes and such, and, if the proposal is scientifically sound, after a précis has been made, will pass it on to a member of the consulting panel. The consulting panel will consist of experts named by the board who are competent professionally to pass upon inventions in various fields, and who will have knowledge as to whether the suggestion submitted has been previously considered and rejected, or whether it is worth while adopting or investigating further. The panel will not meet as a body, and any member will only report on proposals passed to him for an opinion. The board will select the panel from among those competent to serve in our institution, the Department of National Defence, the War Supply Board, the British Mission, and other such organizations. The board itself will only receive those suggestions or inventions which a member of the consulting panel recommends for adoption, trial or further investigation, and it will be the duty of the board of three to see that such suggestions are brought to the competent bodies for action.

I discussed the matter with Colonel Maclachlan and Mr Campbell, and they both think the set-up is sound and are willing and anxious to act on the board.

As I see it, the chief value of the board will not be so much in sieving out suggestions from incompetent people as in passing on the results of research and suggestions made by responsible officers from universities and other institutions. In my opinion, it is imperative not only that all ideas should be thoroughly canvassed, but, if any value is found in them, that they should be cleared promptly to the body which has power and responsibility for action, if any is to be taken.

The work on gauges is progressing favourably, and we have been actually examining gauges since the middle of the month. The volume, while small, is increasing, and our staff is expanding satisfactorily. We have fitted up the room which was used as an instrument museum south of the aeronautical museum,* and now have suitable accommodation for handling a large volume of work efficiently. An arrangement of tables and lighting will permit about 150 examiners to work in this room.

The method of financing the gauge project has been a bit troublesome, but I think I have it worked out satisfactorily now with the British mission† and the Ontario Research Foundation, and everyone seems happy with the solution suggested.

We have, as you know, received a modified request for the scientific personnel which is to be sent to the Admiralty and are in the process of getting lists of suitable candidates. The matter is held up at the moment awaiting the decision of the government as to which department will put up the necessary finances, but I hope this will be solved in the immediate future.

The project which you initiated in [L.E.] Howlett's laboratory is progressing well, and I had a meeting last week with General Elkins, who is anxious to go on with the entire program. As you know, we have the equipment now on order and by spring will be in a position to carry out all the processing and testing in the optical laboratory.

You will be interested to know that the gun sight in Parkin's laboratory‡ is reaching the final stage and is being enamelled today, and will be out for test in the near future. Dr [L.G.] Turnbull reports that it looks like a satisfactory job.

[George J.] Klein has developed an improved slide rule for range calculating, and will be sending you three samples shortly.

The contractor at the new site is a flop and we are having an awful time with him. I have written weekly to the minister and have finally got him to make a formal protest to the minister of Public Works. While the excavation is about completed and a certain amount of concrete work in place, the contractor is obviously inefficient and the job is running badly, with a change of superintendents every few weeks. However, we will keep pounding away and do the best we can.

I understand that your invention,§ being developed for use in

---

*Two large rooms in the basement of the NRC laboratory on Sussex Drive, used before the war as a small aeronautical museum.
†On the inspection of war materials.
‡A gun sight invented by McNaughton to take into account tidal motions.
§The cathode-ray direction finder, a forerunner of radar, invented by McNaughton and Colonel W.A. Steel in 1925.

Henderson's laboratory, is near completion and as soon as the tests are made it will be shipped to England. You will appreciate that under present conditions with the strain on RCAF equipment it has been difficult to get facilities for field testing.

We have been getting quite a lot of publicity these days. The various newspapers have taken still pictures, the National Film Board of Canada has had a publicity man and moving-picture operators in the building for some days, and recently the March of Time people made some interesting pictures which are to be incorporated into a March of Time film covering Canada's war effort.

There is one project on which I have been doing a bit of work, but on which it is difficult to get action. My suggestion is that arrangements should be made for Canada to keep in England an establishment of from twenty-five to fifty scientific workers who would be engaged in a civilian capacity in the various research establishments in England. At the present time, a young man in Canada who wishes to enter any of the services has an opportunity to put his abilities at the disposal of the Empire, but, while there is a real need for our young research workers in the laboratories in England, there is at present no method by which they may be placed there. I have suggested to the minister that it would be an excellent thing if a scheme could be worked out to meet this need, and the Research Council vested with the responsibility of selecting the personnel, placing them in the laboratories in England, and *determining their length of stay*. The scheme would have two aspects. Certain workers might be placed in laboratories in England, where needed, for the duration of the war, and they could undoubtedly make a real contribution, as many of our young men did in the last war. Others could be placed in the various research institutions in England for a time and then brought back to Canada to assist in the direction of research here, to the end that our efforts in Canada would be well directed and effective at all times. The whole scheme seems wise and sound to me, as Canada would not only be making a present contribution of real merit, but we would be assured also that when the war is over, there would return to this country for peace-time activities a number of bright young men who had gained valuable experience by working under the best research brains in England at a time of national emergency and great stimulation. My difficulty is that the scheme is really broader than our own functions; but I do feel that if the proper representations were made from authorities in Britain it would receive sympathetic attention in this country. Perhaps, if you approve, you could plant the idea in appropriate quarters.

You no doubt have heard that Mgr Vachon has been appointed Archbishop Coadjutor of Ottawa. I sent him a note of congratulation on behalf of the council and expressed the hope that his new honours would not mean that he would be unable to continue his services on our council. Up to the present time, I have not had a chance to discuss this phase with him.

I am afraid this is a rambling, disconnected sort of letter, but I have tried to give you information in which I thought you might be interested. I realize naturally that you are very busy, and those of us on this side have derived a great deal of satisfaction in hearing of your manifold activities and of the reception which the division is receiving on the other side. We all know that the future will prove that our pride is well founded.

My wife and I would both like to be remembered to Mrs McNaughton, and the entire staff joins me in sincere best wishes to you and sincere hope for your speedy and safe return to the institution which owes so much to you.

Sincerely yours

C.J. MACKENZIE
Acting President
National Research Council

Aldershot, Hampshire
20 February 1940

Dear Dean Mackenzie:

I have just received and read your letter of 18 January 1940 with the closest attention and interest, and with the deepest satisfaction that under your leadership there has been continuity in the past work of the council and bold venture into new fields, and I am sure that results of great value will come out of your work which will represent a substantial contribution to meet the needs of Canada both for peace and war. I am happy to see that you have been able to bring the chairman of the Privy Council Committee much closer into the picture than I ever was able to and also that Elkins and Maclachlan of the Defence Department and Wallace Campbell of the Supply Board are co-operating fully with you.

As you may imagine, my time here is largely taken up with organization, administration, and training problems, with heavy inroads to satisfy the call for appearances at public and semi-public functions which cannot be refused, and speeches on numerous occasions, some reasonably necessary and some not. This is a most peculiar war, but in the period of waiting for supplies to build up, everything possible must be done to keep the public alive to the purpose for which the British Empire and France have undertaken the vast expenditures of time and effort and resources on which they are now engaged.

So far I have had little opportunity to contact our old friends in scientific research. Apart from Lord Riverdale, the only ones I have seen are those concerned with service problems in the narrow range of direct interest to a division such as survey, flash spotting, and sound ranging, in which fields many of the old group are back on the job.

I have had many proposals to take an interest in this and that new idea which I have had to send elsewhere; I have limited myself to taking a hand in only two projects, the one, the improvement of predicted shooting in the field, which is an old hobby of mine, and the other to press the experiment with the 'core borers.'

In the first I now have, I think, the full co-operation of the School of Artillery, and we should get along with the solution of an acute problem which has been trifled with occasionally during the last twenty or so years. I think the thing which has really wakened people here up is the fact that the Germans are again using air-burst ranging* on an extensive scale and obtaining results which are proving to be very accurate indeed.

In the other, the experiment with the core borer, we have the asset of having one hundred thousand dollars (figures confidential) provided by the Ontario Mining Association, all equipment required, and a specially organized section of [Twelfth Field Company, Royal Canadian Engineers] to offer. Through this we have obtained the co-operation of the Mining Committee of the Council of Scientific and Technical Research of the Ministry of Supply and the RE [Royal Engineering] and Signals Experimental Board, and we have taken on a predetermined program which has already started. Papers on this project are, I think, on file in your office and it would interest you to look them up. Anyway, next time you are in Toronto, I suggest you contact Oliver Hall of Noranda and get him to tell you what he is doing there through his Technical Committee. There is a possibility he may need the co-operation of the Research Council.

*The use of a visible shell burst to estimate where the next shell should be placed.

When I was in France a few weeks ago, I explained the technical possibilities of the core borer at GHQ, and the C-in-C, his chief engineer, and one of the corps commanders amongst others are behind us in pressing this research program; also, we have the support of *some* of the RE [Royal Engineering] officers at the War Office.

[Sir Frederick] Banting and [Major I.M.] Rabinowitch have now gone back to Canada and by this time should have been in touch with you. They carry a precious load of relevant information for the Medical Research Committee and proposals (particularly those made by Rabinowitch in gas warfare) for co-operative work between England and Canada which are worth every consideration and support. If they are proceeded with, there should develop, in these fields an opportunity to commence the project you have outlined, of sending a number of our young scientists over here for employment in British research establishments during the war.

Please give my kindest regards to Mr [Hon W.D.] Euler, to the members of the council and to the staff, and with best wishes to yourself and Mrs Mackenzie, in which my wife joins.

Very sincerely yours

A.G.L. McNaughton

Ottawa
1 March 1940

Dear General McNaughton:

I have been receiving reports of your activities from Sir Frederick Banting and Dr Rabinowitch, both of whom returned home safely. We read a great deal also in the newspapers concerning your activities and those of the First Division, and everyone in Canada is very proud of both.

Feeling that you may find a few leisure moments, I thought I would note down for your information some of the highlights of the work going on here.

When Sir Frederick Banting returned he spent three days in Ottawa and we went thoroughly into all the matters which he had investigated in England. We spent a couple of hours with General Elkins in connection with the chemical-warfare research work and Banting then spent considerable time with Dr Flood and Colonel Morrison. When Rabinowitch got here this week, realizing that the major part of his activities in England seemed to have been in connection with training, I telephoned both General Elkins and General [T.V.] Anderson and had Rabinowitch discuss with General Anderson and Colonel Murchie matters relating to training, and with General Elkins, Colonel [G.P.] Morrison and Dr Flood, matters concerning the investigations and researches on chemical warfare. There is a considerable amount of interest here in both phases of the work and everyone seemed sympathetic and anxious to implement as many of the suggestions as possible. We regard the Committee on Container Proofing as the nucleus of a Porton* and already steps have been taken to enlarge the committee and the scope of the work. The relationships between our laboratories and the MGO's department [Master General of the Ordnance] are almost ideal and I think everyone is highly pleased with the co-operation.

Banting is enthusiastic about aviation medicine and spent two days with me this week going over the proposals for the future. He is anxious that the committee should be reorganized and brought directly under the council and I think that most of the other members of the committee are so inclined.

Our contacts with all parties are on an excellent basis and I think that day by day the government departments and others engaged in the war effort are becoming increasingly aware of the importance of the work of the council. The sort of intimate and effective co-operation which we have always had with the MGO's branch has extended to the other services and departments. As an instance, Admiral Nelles, chief of Naval Staff, called me the other day and said they were in need of a scientist to direct their special investigations in Nova Scotia and elsewhere. He said he felt the best arrangement would be for the National Research Council to engage a man and then he could be seconded for the work with the Navy, the Naval Service to pay his salary and all expenses. Admiral Nelles suggested that the above arrangement would permit the man to feel that he had direct contact with the Research Council and all its facilities while at the same time working on naval problems. I promised the admiral that we would find a man and make all arrangements before the month was out. We have many other contacts with the Naval Service and I think they appreciate what we can do. The same thing is true of the Air Force – of course, from the stand-point of aeronautical engineering such has always been the case, but our contacts with the other phases, particularly the rapidly expanding training scheme, are satisfactory.

*Porton, Wiltshire, was the location of the British Chemical Warfare School.

I have been asked to give several addresses, two of which I am giving in Toronto and Montreal this month, and on every occasion I have taken the opportunity to point out the co-operative nature of our endeavours and stress the essential purpose of the Research Council, namely, to stimulate and co-ordinate research throughout the country and to serve our government departments and industry.

The Inventions Board is working out well and, while it involves considerable work on the part of the junior staff, it brings us directly in contact with all the government departments from the Prime Minister's Office down.

The problems under the special war-appropriation grant are proceeding nicely and it looks as if we would spend most of the money by March 31. We have under way over sixty specific problems under this grant and, while many of them are small studies in the various universities, Henderson's work involves considerable money as do several of the other projects.

The gauge laboratory is well in operation; while the demands have not been excessive to date, we expect them to increase in the near future, and with the set-up we have in the museum I estimate that we can expand our force to 150 without any difficulty. We have the paper organization, the equipment on order, and a trained skeleton organization.

Dr Maass has done valuable work for us in connection with the organization of chemical research. At the present time we have about thirty-six definite chemical researches going on across the Dominion from the Atlantic to the Pacific. Naturally, most of the problems being undertaken at the universities are limited in scope, but already some interesting results have been obtained and the reaction of the chemists throughout the country is excellent. Various industrial laboratories are also working on some of the problems and, of course, work in the NRC laboratories on container proofing,* textiles, leather, laundering, paints, plastics, etc., is going on actively.

In physics, the work in Henderson's laboratory is assuming larger proportions and Boyle, Henderson, and [F.H.] Sanders are all busy on it. A great deal of travelling is required in this work as we are constantly hearing of developments which need to be investigated and reported to the proper bodies in England.

War work in the Biology Division is concentrated on blood storage, and

---

*The development of filter containers for gas masks.

the study of transportation and storage in its relationship to bacon, which is being carried on by Dr [W.H.] Cook.

Parkin is busy as usual and the Aerodynamics Administration Building at the new site is progressing a little more favourably. The steel is nearly all up and the organization seems to be functioning more efficiently. I am enclosing a photograph which will give you some idea of the situation as it was in the later part of February. The contracts for the heating plant have been let and the tenders for the shops are being called.

We were all shocked at the death of Lord Tweedsmuir, particularly so as he had visited the laboratories only a few days before he was taken ill. We were all charmed with him – he was so interested in all the work that was going on here. The last thing he said before he left was that he wanted to come back the next week and go through the aeronautical laboratory. His death was a misfortune for the Empire and I think nearly everyone in Canada felt a sense of personal loss.

I was in Toronto on February 8 and visited the Ontario Research Foundation. Dr Speakman invited me to lunch at Hart House with a group of about fifteen, including Mr Holt Gurney and several of the directors and members of the staff of the foundation and the University of Toronto, and I had an enjoyable time. I think our relationship with the foundation is excellent and I see no reason why it should not remain so. I have worked out the technical and financial arrangements as between the NRC gauge laboratory, the ORF gauge laboratory and the British Supply Board to the mutual satisfaction of all.

The British Supply Board uses our council a great deal in a consulting capacity and, in connection with the inspection of some cable for which they have no trained inspectorate, [B.G.] Ballard has organized a program and farmed out the work to the electrical engineering departments at McGill and Toronto. This is the type of arrangement which you spoke of immediately after war broke out as being desirable from all standpoints and it certainly is working out that way.

I have been busy the last few weeks with activities and engagements both day and night and in about three weeks our next meeting of council will be held – we are planning on taking four days, two for the committee meetings and two for the council meeting itself. So I know I will be very busy until the end of March and probably there will be no let-up until the war is over as it seems that we get busier and busier every week.

I have heard indirectly that Mrs McNaughton has not been well but I do hope she has completely recovered. All the members of the council and the staff mention you frequently and they all wish to be remembered affectionately to you. My wife joins me in extending to you both our very best wishes for the coming year.

Yours sincerely

C.J. Mackenzie

ps – We were worried for a while as to what would happen after March 31, as Parliament was dissolved without any estimates being considered and the election is not to take place until March 26, which probably means that the session will not begin before May. I was particularly concerned about our war projects but a few days ago I took the matter up with the minister and obtained his definite instructions to proceed with all war projects just as if the special war appropriations had been passed. This has relieved us considerably.

Ottawa
12 March 1940

Dear General McNaughton:

Your letter of February 25 reached me today. I have arranged for the thin copper sheets, for which you asked, to be despatched immediately, and I hope that they reach you without delay.

I also received your letter of the twentieth and I appreciate the compliment which you pay us in writing at such length when you must be frightfully busy.

With regard to the core borer, the papers which you mention were forwarded to you at your office in the Fraser Building shortly before you left for England. However, I will get in contact with Mr Oliver Hall, as you suggest, the first time I am in Toronto.

Since writing to you last, things have gone on quite well, and at the present moment Sir Frederick Banting is in town and we are working on the reorganization of the Aviation Committee. The work has gone on very well in Toronto and they have some promising leads which are of interest to the aviation people. They are planning on making a chamber which can be kept at a pressure and temperature corresponding to an altitude of forty thousand feet – that means a pressure of only a few pounds per square inch at a temperature of fifty degrees below zero. There are a large number of problems in this field and Sir Frederick estimates that he will need about $125,000 to carry on for a year. We have been busy the last few days trying to get the money and also trying to get the committee reorganized as an associate committee of the Research Council instead of a committee of the Department of National Defence. We got a resolution through the committee itself to this effect last Saturday. The CAS [Chief of the Air Staff] seems agreeable and the deputy minister I think will agree. If we can do that it will be a great feather in our cap as then we will have practically all the research work of all the three services associated with the Research Council.

I just made the final arrangements with Admiral Nelles yesterday by which the Research Council will take on its strength, on a part-time basis, Doctors [G.H.] Henderson and [J.H.L.] Johnstone of Dalhousie who will have charge of the scientific work of the Navy and who will make the necessary contact between all such work and the National Research Council.

Another interesting development is in connection with the engineering physicists whom we are to send to England. When we started recruiting them, we found that there was some reluctance on the part of the candidates to leave Canada and enter the Old Country services, and I suggested that it would be much more satisfactory if we enlisted these men in the RCNVR [RCN volunteer Reserve] and then despatched them overseas for special duty with the Admiralty. I was surprised when this suggestion was accepted and at the present time the men we send over will all hold commissions in the RCNVR and will be seconded for the duration to the appropriate research stations and service units.

I have also received several letters from Sir Richard Tute regarding an invention in the States by Dr Marcel Wallace, whose laboratory Dr [J.T.] Henderson plans to visit in the near future. Sir Richard is insisting that I send the correspondence to you. I am therefore enclosing copies of his letters, but you will appreciate that we are keeping closely in touch with this work and will take the appropriate steps if action is required. Unfortunately, I cannot tell Sir Richard Tute anything about it.

The election is in full swing, with voting two weeks from today, but up to the present time there does not seem to be a great deal of heat in the campaign and it looks as if the present government would be returned. Of course, elections are proverbially uncertain.

Our committee and council meetings will be held on Monday, Tuesday, Wednesday, and Thursday of next week.

I was a little bit concerned about our work under the special war appropriation as, by Act, the grant expires on March 31 and, unlike the regular work of the council, we were faced with the problem of giving notice to all our employees under this grant and stopping the provision of equipment for future delivery. However, I went to the minister and pointed out to him the unfortunate consequences that would arise if we sent notices all over the country to the effect that all work on special war projects would have to terminate on March 31, which we would have to do to protect ourselves unless we could get assurance from the government that, regardless of what happened, necessary provision would be made. The minister saw the situation immediately and gave me instructions to proceed with all the work just as if our estimates for the special war appropriation had been passed. This relieved the condition and we are going ahead at full speed.

I spoke at the Engineering Institute in Montreal last Thursday and I think that group was impressed with the work which the Research Council is doing under the war conditions. I go to Toronto to do the same thing on the fourth of April and, while these activities are time consuming and tiresome, I feel that the set-up and work of the council is something of which the general public should be aware, and if we can get the general public's backing now it should make things easier after the war.

I will write to you again as soon as the proceedings of the next council meeting are available or whenever anything of interest happens.

Sir Frederick, who is in my office, joins me in sending kindest regards to you and Mrs McNaughton.

Sincerely yours

C.J. MACKENZIE

Ottawa
9 April 1940

Dear General McNaughton:

I trust that you have received by this time the copper sheets which you requested in your letter of February 25. We, unfortunately, did not have any of them here but I asked Mr Gill to get in touch with the Anaconda

American Brass Company Limited, secure a few sample sheets, and have them forwarded to you.

Mr Gill is now at the War Supply Board assisting in the work in connection with gauges. Some time ago, I had a communication from Mr Wallace Campbell who wanted to get Gill seconded to his staff to assist Dr Robb on the gauge work. I spoke to Gill, who had previously discussed the matter with Robb, and as he was anxious to undertake the work I agreed to the transfer for the time being. I told Mr Campbell, however, that in my opinion Gill had particular abilities which should be of great value in an organization such as the War Supply Board, and that if they found a really useful place for him we would permit him to stay but if he were not given important duties we would probably recall him. At the present time we are considering an arrangement whereby Gill's Section on Codes and Specifications will write special specifications for the War Supply Board. They would not be official Dominion government purchasing standard specifications but would, I think, be useful during the war.

We had four busy days from the eighteenth to the twenty-first of March with our committee and council meetings. The minutes are being prepared and Mr Eagleson will send you a copy as soon as they are available. Much of the time was taken up with consideration of our war activities and we had prepared full reports on the various projects. I think that the council was well pleased with the progress that is being made.

Some weeks ago, Dr Newton informed me that he had been offered the position of dean of Agriculture at Alberta, which was made vacant by Dean Howe's death. We discussed the matter at some length and I pointed out to him that the position, as such, was not comparable in importance to the position which he already held, but he said that for some time he had been wishing to get back to university work and that if he did not make a move now it would probably be too late in a few years. I think Mrs Newton is anxious to go back to Edmonton and has, no doubt, influenced his decision materially. I considered the whole problem carefully and as I did not think it proper for the council to fill this position in your absence, or at least without some conversations with you on the matter, I suggested to council that, instead of accepting Dr Newton's resignation, we grant him a year's leave of absence without pay. This has been done and it will enable us to go through the next year without any pressure being applied to fill the vacancy. I have decided to let Doctors W.H. Cook and J.G. Malloch carry the administrative load for the time being at least. Dr Newton thinks highly of Cook and I am sure would recommend him as his successor, but whether Cook is sufficiently mature for this position I am not at present prepared to say, although I have no doubts as to his very marked intellectual ability. However, a year will give us time to observe, and by that time you will be able to offer an opinion as to whether or not we should proceed to fill this position. In the meantime, I think the arrangement will work very well.

Dr Flood is in uniform now and while he is going to remain in charge of our laboratory, as before, he will be going to England presently to exchange information and experiences with the people at Porton. I am planning on having Dr Maass go over about the middle of May in order to acquaint the scientists in England with the work which we have done here and obtain information from them and solicit their views as to the most appropriate chemical problems to prosecute in Canada. Dr Rabinowitch told me yesterday that, as you probably have been informed, steps are being taken to implement your suggestions regarding the training for gas warfare in Canada.

The papers suggest that Mr [Hon N.M.] Rogers, the minister of National Defence, will be in England shortly and as you will, no doubt, have many opportunities to discuss affairs with him, I was wondering if you would care to mention our problem in connection with the despatching of scientists to England. I have already mentioned the matter generally to Mr Rogers but it occurs to me that a word from you might be the means of our getting this difficult problem solved. I mentioned in a previous letter the difficulty which we were having in getting engineer-physicists for the Admiralty. Most of our young people, apparently, are not keen to go to England and enter the services there due to the fact that there are many drawbacks in connection with income taxes, future pensions, and treatment. As soon as it was arranged that the engineers who were to take commissions could be enlisted in the RCNVR, we had little difficulty in obtaining the personnel; they will go to England as members of the RCNVR and be seconded to the RN for duties as originally planned. We are, however, having difficulty in getting research workers for the civilian stations, and the difficulty is largely due to the fact that these men, most of whom are now occupying good positions, cannot see their way clear to accepting the British offer. A job at £630 per year looks attractive at first, but, when they consider that about fifty per cent will be taken away in income tax and that the worker will be under the jurisdiction of the department of another government, the uncertainties make the position seem unattractive. I, personally, am quite sure that there is need for a number of Canadian scientists in England to work in the various research stations there, and I am equally convinced that it will be in the interests of Canada to have, after the war, a group of young men so trained and available for service in Canada, but at the present time it is almost impossible for us to get anywhere with the project. Both Sir Frederick and Dr Rabinowitch brought back word that Canadian workers were needed and would be welcomed at the research stations at Porton and elsewhere, but our minister takes the viewpoint that if these men are needed, there should be an official request from the British government and this position is, I think, understandable. I prepared a memorandum which I presented to the minister, a copy of which I am enclosing, and while the details might be modified I think the general plan is sound. I feel if Mr Rogers, while in England, could be convinced that such a contribution on the part of Canada would be welcome and of great benefit to all parties, that we might be able to get something done, and I am sure that if you think well of the scheme there is no one who would have greater influence in urging it upon Mr Rogers.

There is another matter which I think someone should urge upon Mr Rogers and the government and that is the advantage of having a scientific liaison officer attached to either Mr Massey's office or to the Military Headquarters in London. One of the greatest difficulties we have is to secure free transmission of information between Canada and the Old Country. We have tried many channels and while some of them appear to work we are never certain. A great deal has been done under the auspices of the council on chemical work and it seems impossible to be sure that there is an effective transfer of information to the authoritative sources in England. It is for this reason that I am having Dr Maass visit England during May. It occurred to me that, if the Canadian Government would maintain a scientist, nominated by and responsible to the National Research Council, in London as a liaison officer between the scientific agencies in Canada and Great Britain, it would be profitable for all concerned.

The election now being over we hope to get on with the serious business of the war and, while no announcements have been made with regard to financial arrangements for the carrying out of the council's business until Parliament meets, we are not worrying and are proceeding on the basis that everything will be taken care of. There has been no decision as to how aviation medical research will be carried out, whether under an associate committee of the Research Council or a special committee of the Department of National Defence. However, we should shortly get some information on the subject.

I have just heard that Sir Frederick is likely to go to England to take charge of the research laboratory of the Canadian Red Cross Hospital at Taplow. I cannot blame him for wanting to go but his absence will, I feel, have a serious effect on the support which will be forthcoming for the research work at Toronto on aviation medicine.

I was in Toronto last week for the purpose of addressing the Toronto branch of the Engineering Institute of Canada and I spent an interesting day with Sir Frederick at the Banting Institute and was much impressed with the work that is being done there. They have a decompression chamber which can simulate pressure conditions at forty to fifty thousand feet and they hope soon to be able to operate under temperature conditions of -40 to $-50°F$. I took a flight in the decompressor and realized that I would be a good subject for research as at high altitudes I had considerable trouble with my ears.

Everything is going along nicely here and from the news we receive I gather that your First Division is rapidly rounding into first-class battle condition. We follow your moves with great interest and all the members of the staff wish to be remembered to you.

With best wishes and kind regards to both Mrs McNaughton and yourself.

Sincerely yours

C.J. MACKENZIE

Aldershot, Hampshire
27 March 1940

Dear Dean Mackenzie:

A few days ago I had a discussion with Mr A. Caldwell, a member of the Institution of Naval Architects and a member and past president of the Institution of Mechanical Engineers, on the subject of towing tanks, and I told him of Tupper's work in connection with the study of 'Boundary Wall Interference.' He was much interested and I promised to write to you for copies of Tupper's reports so that I could send them on to him.

I would be much obliged if you could let me have these papers and also a note as to the dimensions and particulars of the new tank which we have planned for installation on the Montreal Road property in due course.

Everything goes well with the division and we are just now in the midst of the detailed inspections of the units following the completion of individual training.

With kindest regards and best wishes.

Very sincerely yours

A.G.L. McNaughton

Ottawa
20 April 1940

Dear General McNaughton:

I just received your letter of March 27 and have obtained copies of Tupper's article on the effect of the basin walls on ship-model tests. I am enclosing two copies of this paper.

The proposed new model basin on the Montreal Road property will be 600 feet long, 25 feet wide, and 10 feet deep. It is planned to equip the basin with two carriages, a slow-speed car for ship-model tests (maximum speed of about fifteen feet per second) and a high-speed car for seaplane tests (maximum speed of about thirty-seven feet per second). The plans of the building, of course, are well along but the detailed design of the carriage equipment has not been completed.

Everything is going along quite nicely here. It looks now as if the Committee on Aviation Medical Research would get a grant of $109,000 and the work be done under an associate committee of the Research Council. I have been following unofficially the course of the proposals we made through the various official channels and, yesterday, when the new acting deputy minister of Defence for Air, Mr [J.S.] Duncan of Toronto, phoned me about the matter and I offered to go down and see him, explain the advantages of the proposed arrangement, and give him some idea of the importance of the work, I left with the opinion that he would recommend the scheme as drafted.

I have some misgivings about the way the gauge testing is working out. Our laboratory is thoroughly equipped – R.H. Field has just returned from a three months' trip in England where he worked with and observed the methods used in the NPL [National Physical Laboratory] and Woolwich, and is probably today the best-informed person on the American continent as to current English practice. At Toronto the laboratory is being run by a young man with an engineering degree, only a few weeks' special training in Quebec, and no great knowledge of metrology. There is doubt in my mind that the methods and techniques are comparable in the two institutions. It would have been far better I think if we had been responsible for the whole thing but I understand how it all happened and nothing can be done about that now. I think probably we can get around the situation in a diplomatic way without any trouble. I had an informal talk with Major-General [R.F.] Lock and told him that, as far as we were concerned, the work had to be first-class, and according to the standards which we knew were being maintained in England, if we were to remain in the picture. He was unaware of the situation and very much of my way of thinking.

You will, by now, have received all the first-hand information about the Canadian picture from the minister and Major-Generals [V.W.] Odlum and Elkins. We, in turn, will look forward to hearing some first-hand information about your activities when the delegation returns.

I have made arrangements for Dr Maass to go to England about the middle of May to make a thorough study of the chemical-research situation there and to take from Canada information on the considerable amount of work that has been done here.

I have also arranged that Dr George Henderson of Dalhousie, who is temporarily on our staff and seconded to the Navy for special work, will go about the same time and do the same thing in the various fields of physics, in which we are mutually interested. We will acquaint him with details of Dr J.T. Henderson's work here and have him bring back a report on the latest developments there, which will assure us that our work is being done effectively and is in step with latest developments in England.

With kindest personal regards.

Sincerely yours

C.J. MACKENZIE

Aldershot, Hampshire
11 April 1940

Dear Dean Mackenzie:

I have your letters of 1 March and 12 March 1940 to answer, both of which

I have read with the greatest interest indeed and with the deepest satisfaction in the forceful leadership which you are giving to the council in the many and varied new activities which must be undertaken in the service of Canada and of the Empire at this time.

I am very pleased that Banting's project for the reorganization of the Committee on Aviation Medicine is going through and that there will be an extension of this work. The reduced-pressure chamber for study of physical conditions at high altitude will be a valuable piece of apparatus. Recent developments (very secret) indicate the increasing importance of flight at the highest altitudes, particularly for fighter-type aircraft.

Please give my best wishes to Henderson and Johnstone of Dalhousie on their appointment to take charge of scientific work for the RCN. I think the commissioning of the young scientists in our service and their seconding to the RN is an admirable solution of the problem of handling the engineering physicists whom you are to send here.

As regards the Wallace invention and the correspondence with Sir Richard Tute – the only thing I felt I could do was to write Watson Watt and send the papers to him. This I did under cover of letter dated 10 April 1940, a copy of which I mailed to you. In this you will see that I suggested that he should write to you direct if he had any interest in the matter.

The experiments with the core borer are going splendidly and tomorrow we are giving a demonstration before Lord Cadman and the other members of the joint committee set up by the Engineering and Signals Board and the Ministry of Supply.

Everything goes well with the division and our training is progressing satisfactorily.

With kindest regards to all.

Very sincerely yours

A.G.L. McNaughton

Ottawa
4 May 1940

Dear General McNaughton:

I just received your letter of April 11 and under separate cover a copy of your letter to Mr Watson Watt in connection with the Wallace invention, backed by Sir Richart Tute. I might say that Dr Boyle went to New York last week for the specific purpose of investigating the Wallace invention and he feels that it is of sufficient interest and importance to be brought formally to the attention of the interested parties. He is consequently preparing a report which he will send to Messrs Watson Watt and [H.G.] Gough.

We have been having another session with the estimates. An order came through last week that all estimates for non-war purposes must be reduced to the 1936–37 level. This policy, I think, is a sound one for most departments but, of course, is entirely impracticable for us. I pointed out to Mr Euler and to Treasury Board officials that the National Research Council laboratories were formally opened in 1932 without adequate staff or equipment, and it was not until 1935–36 that a real start was made to equip them properly. Consequently, if our estimates were reduced to the 1936–37 level, the total appropriation would not be enough to pay the salaries of our regular staff. The thing that the official mind finds difficulty in understanding is why we cannot cut our pre-war costs materi-ally when we are receiving about four hundred thousand dollars for war projects and when eighty per cent of our activities have a war bearing. I think, however, that we were able to present a convincing argument: I pointed out to them that the money which is being spent on war projects is being spent for junior professional and subprofessional staff and special equipment; that the expert direction and supervision is given by our permanent staff, which also, of course, directs other, civil projects; that if our permanent organization were disrupted it would mean that the various fighting services would have to set up complete laboratories themselves with expensive directing officers, and that, instead of spend-ing four hundred thousand a year on special war projects, they would probably be faced with an expenditure five or six times that amount. We have a good case and do not intend to let the vital structure be destroyed. Everyone with whom I have spoken to date has been convinced of our worthiness and we feel that after making quite respectable reductions in some of the essentially peace-time assisted research grants, and paring the laboratory estimates for new equipment, we will have no difficulty. If it comes to a show-down I will ask for the privilege of appearing with a delegation of heavy artillery to make a final stand, but I don't anticipate that this will be necessary.

The aviation-medical problem has been solved – an Order in Council has been passed asking the council to set up an associate committee and granting us $109,000 for the work.

Professor A.V. Hill, who is at present at the embassy in Washington on some liaison work, visited Ottawa this week. We enjoyed him very much and the results of his visit will be useful to our cause. I presume you have met Hill and will recall that he is secretary of the Royal Society, a Nobel Prize winner in medicine, a professor of physiology at London, a member of Parliament for Cambridge University, and a first-class physicist and electrical engineer who has done a great deal of work on instrument design in connection with artillery and aviation – I think that it is in this latter capacity that he is in America. He is an extraordinarily fine man and one of the ablest I have ever met. We got a lot done while he was here, and the first thing which I was able to do was to prevent him from taking a course which would have been unfortunate. He knows Air Vice-Marshal L.D.D. McKean, who has taken Sir H.R.M. Brooke-Popham's place in connection with the Empire Air Training Scheme, and Hill had suggested that McKean might take on in a liaison capacity in connection with aviation medical research a friend of his who is a very able scientist in physics and physiology and, incidentally, a pilot with 1600 hours in the air. This young chap is in Best's laboratory at Toronto and is anxious to get on war work but apparently has not been used to date. I pointed out to Dr Hill and Air Marshal McKean that such a step, instead of providing a good liaison, as they thought, would do the reverse; that, in Canada, we have in the National Research Council what is really a combination of a large number of institutions in Great Britain; that we are doing the scientific work for the Air Force, the Army and the Navy; and that there was no difficulty in obtaining effective liaison with any of the work being done; moreover, if they established a separate scientific service, which in any way could be construed as criticism of the Committee on Aviation Medicine, it might destroy confidence in the broad National Research Council set-up which was the vital thing for all of us to maintain. Hill saw the situation immediately and cancelled arrangements by wire within an hour.

He was generally appreciative of our efforts at the National Research Council, and by the time he left was full of admiration for what Canada was doing. Dr Maass and Dr [J.B.] Collip came up for a day and I gave a luncheon, to which I also invited Sir Gerald Campbell. As you know, we have felt that if we could have a man of Hill's caliber resident in Canada who could act as a liaison officer and effect an immediate channel to the scientific heads in the Old Country, it would materially aid us. I threw out the suggestion that if we could have some such man attached to Sir Gerald's staff, either formally or informally, he could be of great assistance to everyone. Hill immediately agreed, suggesting that no one but a top-ranking man should be sent, and Sir Gerald started the wheels moving within twenty-four hours. Whether or not it will be successful, I do not know, but we all hope so.

The next day Dr Hill and I lunched with Lieutenant-Colonel Greenley. We had more discussions about general matters and I think that Hill's testimony as to the value of the organization which you and others have been able to build will do a lot to make future co-operation here more active.

Professor Hill will be returning to England in a few weeks and I have asked him to make a point of calling on you, if possible, as I assured him that your interest in scientific matters had not been dulled by your active participation in military affairs.

As I have told you, Dr Maass is leaving for England soon, and we have also arranged for Professor Henderson of Dalhousie to go along to investigate matters of particular interest to the Navy. We have had a further communication from the latter service and negotiations are now under way to establish the same type of service on the Pacific as we have on the Atlantic.

The news from Norway these days is not very cheerful but that, I suppose, is historically true to form, as it seems to take a peaceful nation a longer time to get into action, and a gentleman is always at a tactical disadvantage when dealing with a gangster.

With kindest regards and best wishes from the council and the staff.

Sincerely yours

C.J. MACKENZIE

Aldershot, Hampshire
22 May 1940

Dear Dean Mackenzie:

This morning I have your letter of 4 May 1940, and I find on looking back on my file that, in the stress of affairs here, I have neglected to answer your other letters of 9 April and 20 April 1940, for which please accept my sincerest apologies.

The copper sheet which you kindly sent forward has now been received and turned over to Major Harold Hemming at the Survey School, Larkhill, Salisbury Plain, for his experiments in connection with the preparation of non-warping map boards for use by the Field Survey organization and flash spotters. I think it is exactly what he required and we are all much indebted to you and Mr Gill for your trouble in making it available.

As regards the Wallace invention,* I sent the papers along to Watson Watt and I will write him again today telling him that he may shortly expect a further report on the subject from Dr Boyle through you. Watson Watt is a busy man these days but somehow or other he seems to find time to deal with everything, so you may expect that full value will be taken from any information that Dr Boyle sends forward.

I am pleased to see that you have opened a bold defensive against any attempt to destroy the council's organization through an undue cutting down of the appropriations. In point of actual fact, it is my considered opinion that if the council does not continue to be adequately supported, then it will not satisfy the needs of the service departments and they will set up a research organization of their own with consequent heavy duplications in supervisory staff, equipment, etc. The net result would be the multiplication, several fold, in overhead expenditure, and a lessening of the scientific output due to lack of someone with a broad view to co-ordinate, and with a great waste of time all round. Further, while I believe that we have plenty of junior workers of the right calibre available, I doubt that our supply of thoroughtly experienced scientific men for general supervision and administration is anything more than barely adequate, and then only if they are used for the things which they alone are capable of doing.

I am pleased to hear that Banting's proposition in respect to the Associate Committee on Aviation Medical Research has been approved and that the matter is in hand with sufficient funds to make a start at any rate.

I have never had the pleasure of meeting Professor A.V. Hill, but I have heard a good deal about him and am looking forward to seeing him when he returns to England. Also, I am looking forward to seeing Dr Maass and Professor [George] Henderson when they arrive and you may be sure that I will do everything in my power to help them establish their own contacts over here.

These are anxious days and we face many difficulties but, true to history, the British people both in government circles and in the public are taking things calmly. The worse the news, the more they are pulling

*To do with radar.

themselves together for a supreme effort. I have nothing but admiration for them all.

Our own forces are now in fine shape as regards the personnel but we still have some way to go before we have our proper complement of supplies and equipment. It has been, as you may imagine, unfortunate to say the least that we have not been able to make ourselves of use in the line of battle up to date.

With kindest regards to yourself and Mrs Mackenzie, in which my wife joins, and with best wishes to members of the council and all our staff.

Very sincerely yours

per A.G.L. McNaughton
(absent on duty)

Ottawa
17 June 1940

Dear General McNaughton:

I received your letter of May 22 which was apparently written just before your eventful trip to Flanders. First let me say that we feel highly complimented that in the midst of all your work and anxiety you should find time and pleasure in turning your thoughts to the work of the council. As you say, these are anxious days and there are many difficulties, but I think the people on this side of the Atlantic are at last thoroughly awakened. Our only hope is that it is not too late. It seems tragic that those who have tried to prevent catastrophes for years are usually the ones who have to bear the brunt of the consequences, but fortunately good soldiers look forward and do not concern themselves overmuch with what might have been done.

You are probably as well informed about news in Canada as we are, but I do think that at last the war has become a reality and as you advised many months ago, thinking now is more in terms of men, machines, tanks, aeroplanes, supplies, and power, than in terms of figures and entries in international ledgers and bank accounts.

Mr Rogers's untimely death was quite a shock – I think he died a soldier's death. [Hon J.L.] Ralston has taken over Defence, probably what should have been done from the start.

22 May, 17 June 1940

THE
UNIVERSITY OF WINNIPEG
PORTAGE & BALMORAL
WINNIPEG, MAN.   R3B 2E9
CANADA

39

The news today is disturbing and we all wonder where you are. While there has been no official intimation at all, there is a general feeling that the Canadians may be in France in the thick of it, and you and the officers and men of the division are constantly in the minds of all the members of the old corps left in Canada and a host of other friends and admirers.

I feel diffident about telling you of what is going on at the council at this time, as our efforts seem so unimportant compared with your activities, but perhaps it will be a relaxation, if you ever have a spare moment, to hear what is being done.

I got our estimates through Treasury Board without any difficulty and had the privilege of appearing before the full board on two occasions. There was no disposition to question our revised estimates after I had assured them that we had done everything possible to meet the government's desire to cut down normal peace-time expenditures, but that we could not recommend any reductions which would seriously destroy the fabric of the council's organization. It was gratifying to realize that the government appreciates the work that the council is doing and I think that at no time in its history has the council stood higher in the regard of the people who are really doing things in this country. This is largely due to your personal success in making close and effective contacts with the services and industrial leaders of the country.

During the crisis in Flanders and just after Mr Euler had resigned his portfolio and Mr [Hon James Angus] MacKinnon had taken over, an Order in Council came through placing all wartime appointments under the Civil Service Commission. The Order in Council was not directed against us in any sense but the result was alarming, as we found our wartime activities, where we needed flexibility, encircled with restrictions that were much more burdensome than those on our peace-time ac- tivities. I hesitated to go to Treasury Board at that moment, as Parliament was just opening, the situation in Flanders was very serious, everyone was working long hours and was tired and on edge. I felt that if I tried to get an interview to explain our situation it might do more harm than good. Instead I went directly to the Civil Service Commission, put the situation fairly before them, told them that we had no objection to working with them but that the Order just would not work. Mr Bland was most sym- pathetic, admitted our contention immediately and offered to take the initiative in getting it corrected. He interviewed the Finance minister, wrote a letter requesting that the Order as put forward be not applicable to the Research Council, and all the civil service commissioners signed it. I then took it to Mr MacKinnon who signed it and it was passed through

Treasury Board the next morning, so that we got over that stumbling block.

The work in the gauge laboratory is developing rapidly and thanks to your anticipation we are in fairly good shape. [R.H.] Field has a good organization set up in one of the old museum halls, and we can expand our staff rapidly to about 150 and if necessary work in three shifts. We are now trying to see if we cannot have the organization run entirely as a Canadian one, which would give us more flexibility.

The optical-glass situation is developing as you anticipated and the same board that was not interested last October is now feeling concerned. Fortunately, we have the nucleus of a laboratory established and can develop it.

Ballard at the present time is busy on matters in connection with naval protection at Halifax, and he is doing the consulting work, designing and writing specifications, and purchasing all equipment for mine sweepers at Halifax.

I have just received a letter from Colonel Maclachlan stating that a start will probably be made soon for the manufacture of Asdic* equipment in Canada, and he asked if we could give space in our building for the secret assembling work. I do not know where we will find the space but I have told him that we will accommodate him.

Gill has gone to the Department of Munitions and Supply and is now assistant to the director of Production. I permitted him to go because I felt that his energy, enthusiasm, and forcefulness would be useful in an organization that was plowing new furrows. He is happy, doing excellent work, and still keeps in touch with his work here.

The Gauge-Production Section of the Department of Munitions and Supply would like to have the services of van Winsen, who has had much experience in production. If I feel that his services are more useful to the country there than here I will let him go.

[Frank] Peto has developed a strain of beets which may have an important bearing at the present time, as all the countries which formerly exported beet seed to Canada, America, and Great Britain are now in enemy hands and the situation may become critical. It seemed necessary to try to develop this matter more quickly than could be done through the normal routes and we have worked out a good arrangement with Buckerfield's Limited of Vancouver to develop the project immediately

*Device for detecting submarines by echoes of sound waves; from the initials of the Allied Submarine Detection Investigation Committee (UK), set up during World War I.

on a commercial scale in British Columbia; Peto will have charge of the development work there and we have given him two years' leave of absence without pay.

As I intimated to you before, Dr Newton is now in Alberta, having taken over the position of dean of Agriculture there, but as far as we are concerned he is on leave of absence and the work here is being conducted on that basis.

We got the Aviation Medical Research Committee organized with a strong personnel; the actual work is well under way and I think the results will be useful.

Professor A.V. Hill was here again on May 31 on his way back to England and was much concerned over the fact that the scientific facilities in Canada and the USA were not being used by the British to anywhere near the extent they might be. He was returning to England in order to deal with this matter, as cable communication is not very effective in such cases. He said he would try to get an interview with you and I do hope that will be possible.

Parkin is much interested in the proposal to construct fighting aircraft of wood. He feels strongly that we have the resources in timber and plywood here which would be readily available and that the construction would involve artisans and industries not now used to the limit. He thinks that such craft could be constructed cheaper and more rapidly and that they would be both safe and serviceable; also, that the life of a modern plane is so short anyway that the relatively long life of a metal craft would not be an important factor. He prepared a memorandum which I sent to the Department of National Defence and the Department of Munitions and Supply. A copy was also handed to Hill. At the present time there is no indication as to what will happen.

I have seen General Elkins many times since his return and of course see Flood almost daily. They both brought back reports of you and the division; we were all delighted to hear that you were in good physical condition and that the division is in fighting trim.

Everyone at the council wishes to be remembered to you and you have the affection and good wishes of all. My wife joins me in sending best wishes to you and Mrs McNaughton.

Sincerely yours

C.J. MACKENZIE

Ottawa
25 July 1940

Dear General McNaughton:

We were all most delighted when your promotion was announced and while I know the First Division will be sorry to lose its original commander, they will probably be the first to realize that your abilities and services cannot be confined within limited spheres when the stakes are so high.

Much has happened here since I last wrote. The prosecution of the war is on an entirely different basis. It is no longer a perfunctory war and the thinking is now as you recommended at the beginning – in terms of aeroplanes, tanks, men, and machines and not in terms of dollars. Today money is the only thing which can be obtained promptly for any real war purpose. The sad thing is that if we had had available over the past ten or fifteen years a small fraction of the amount now being spent, probably the present tragedy would have been prevented.

Last week I called a special meeting of the council to consider several important matters that had arisen since the June meeting in which you may be interested. I will note them down briefly.

About three weeks ago Mr Duncan, acting deputy minister of National Defence for Air, phoned me that he was calling a meeting to discuss how certain monies which had been contributed to the government might best be spent. At the meeting were present Mr R.A.C. Henry representing Mr [C.D.] Howe, Mr [H.L.] Keenleyside representing Dr [O.D.] Skelton, Colonel [Alan A.] Magee representing Colonel Ralston and one or two others. Mr Duncan explained that John Eaton and Sir Edward Beatty had each offered about a quarter of a million dollars as a contribution to Canada's war effort. Mr Duncan thought that instead of putting the money into the general revenue it would be better if it could be allocated to specific projects and the various people present at the meeting were asked to suggest suitable projects. After several suggestions were made, I was called upon and presented briefly the way in which the council had been working, showing them that in all the projects such as equipping the gauge laboratory, preparing for the manufacture of optical glass, erection of the Aeronautical Building, work on radio, chemical engineering, etc., we had anticipated the nation's needs by several months. I pointed out that had we not so functioned, it would be almost impossible at the present time to equip laboratories such as the gauge department and that conditions would be very serious. In about ten minutes all other projects were discarded and it was decided to suggest to the donors that they make their contributions to the National Research Council for war technical developments.

I met representatives of the donors, Mr John Eaton Jr and Mr Armstrong, representing Sir Edward, two or three days later and they were also enthusiastic about our problem.

A few days ago Sir Edward Beatty called personally at my office and we had a discussion for about an hour. I think he was very much in favour of the project, although he said that it was difficult to make some of his directors and business friends believe that the work of the research institutions was of immediate value. Before going, however, he did say that he would do everything he could to help the project on and he even suggested that he would personally approach companies like International Nickel, Noranda, and Consolidated Smelters, to see if they would not raise a fund to take care of all the special war research that we were doing. While I don't think there will be any difficulty in getting money from the government to do things which need to be done, I do feel that if we had the formal support of groups such as I have mentioned, it would be a great compliment to the council.

There is another phase which I think is equally interesting. Perhaps you know the way in which the Department of Munitions and Supply is developing under Mr Howe. He is gradually surrounding himself with a group of prominent go-getting businessmen who are determined to win the war at any cost. A short time ago I met Mr Woodward informally, and during our conversation I told him that it was strange that while the services of the Department of National Defence made constant use of our facilities, the Department of Munitions and Supply did not seem to know much about us. He immediately said he would come up the next day, and in the last three weeks he has visited the council three times. I have also been called in at conferences and meetings in Mr Howe's office where matters of construction and development were being discussed and think at the present time the Department of Munitions and Supply is very much impressed with the contributions which the Research Council is making.

When it was decided to undertake the manufacture of optical glass, the matter of how the organization should be set up gave us all some concern. It was first suggested that an associate committee, headed by General Elkins and myself with representatives from the Department of Munitions and Supply, and Dr Howlett, might be organized for that purpose. The next suggestion was that the device of incorporating a company with stock one hundred per cent Government owned might be used and that to the board of directors the above-mentioned personnel would be named. While this discussion was going on we were considering the possibility of having to go into the manufacture of [J.T.] Henderson's radio equipment, Asdics, special equipment for the Navy, fine chemicals, etc., and it was suggested to Mr Woodward and Mr Howe that perhaps the best scheme would be to form a comprehensive company under which could be set up departments dealing with such projects. ... This company has now been formed, I understand, and a gentleman by the name of [George W.] Sweny from Vancouver appointed managing director or president. All the details have not been worked out but I think the scheme will be efficient.*

I was somewhat disturbed about the Research Council getting into manufacturing as such. It is true that many of our people would no doubt develop business ability and they do know the technical aspects; however, there is always a danger in handing over business administration to such groups. I was therefore much interested in having developments such as the above take place for, while we control the technical phases now, a management experienced in business matters will attend to the strictly administrative features.

There is some discussion now as to the personnel of the board of directors. General Elkins was to be on the directorate but he has raised the question as to whether an officer of the Department of National Defence should serve in this capacity. It was at one time suggested that I should be president of the company but I refused that and suggested that I was not at all anxious even to be on the directorate, and that probably the best arrangement would be to form a small directorate of businessmen with an active managing director or president, then set up an advisory group of representatives from the three fighting services and the council which would be responsible for placing the precise needs and technical details before the directors. In turn, each of the departments such as optical glass would be administered by a technical officer probably drawn from our council and an advisory group of officers familiar with the details of the particular product. I expect that the general matter of manufacturing will develop rapidly and, no matter what the formal arrangement is, a great deal of the work and the most important phases will fall on the Research Council.

In consideration of all the work which is descending upon us and the activities that are spreading across the country, I asked the council to

*The company was Research Enterprises Limited; for the political rationale behind REL, see the epilogue, pp. 2–3.

approve of the appointment of Dr Maass as a special assistant to me, and I think that the government will so appoint him. Dr Maass is and has been working full time for the council for some time. He gave up teaching at McGill early this year and ever since May has done nothing but look after the researches in chemistry which are being conducted in the various universities and institutions in Canada. He is an extraordinarily valuable man. He was upset about the lack of action before we got into the war but now he is simply calm, determined, and does the job which is immediately before him in a very efficient manner. He is working up to sixteen hours every day. I was sorry that Maass did not see you when he was in England, but it was at a time when you were particularly busy and the situation was critical. He expects to go to England again before the summer is out and perhaps he will have better luck next time.

It looks as if we might be getting somewhere with the wooden aeroplane. There is a development which has taken place in the States which is really quite marvellous. The aeroplane fuselages and wings are made with plywood by a process of moulding. Forms are made for half a fuselage, veneer in strips is placed against the forms in three layers and forced together by means of a bag which presses against the inside surface. The veneer strips are coated on both sides with a plastic and the whole assembly is run into a tank and subjected to a pressure of forty to fifty pounds of steam. In fifty minutes the assembly comes out and it is a marvellous-looking job. The equipment required in the shops is ridiculously small. A few saws and wood-working instruments are all one sees. It is estimated that the complete fuselages and wings can be turned out very rapidly and we are all enthusiastic. I sent Parkin, Gallay, [R.D.] Hiscocks and Sqn Ldr Rees to visit the Vidal Plant in New Jersey and see it in operation. They came back much impressed. The president of the firm told them that in sixty days they would turn out three assemblies, complete except for engine, of any aeroplane type the Canadian government desired; that they would have two of them tested for destruction under static load and one given a trial flight test, and that if these units did not live up to every specification, there would be no expense to the government. Parkin saw complete planes being turned out for the United States Army and he says that the planes are very light and that the cost should be only a fraction of the ordinary metal planes. When Parkin got back I telephoned Mr Ralph Bell who has been appointed head of Mr Howe's aeroplane company and he immediately came down and heard the story. He was very enthusiastic, and said he would immediately get in touch with Mr Vidal and arrange to have trial orders placed, and would take steps to have the offer of three planes for test accepted. Meanwhile, we are going on with our work in plastics and plywoods in case the matter develops rapidly and hope to be of some service should large-scale developments take place.

Last week I invited the new Governor General, the Earl of Athlone, to visit the council. He immediately accepted and came three days later. To our surprise Her Royal Highness, the Princess Alice, and the Lady May Abel-Smith accompanied him. I think the visit was reasonably successful and they seemed pleased.

The corner-stone of the Aerodynamics Building was properly laid this morning and one of the highlights was your cable, which arrived just in time for the ceremony. I read it during the proceedings and it was enthusiastically received; we all felt that it was a great compliment to receive such a message from you at the present time when your days must be so fully occupied with matters of the greatest importance. I am sending you the official invitation. The Hon Mr MacKinnon was to have been chairman, but at eleven o'clock last night he found that with the initiation of morning sittings he was on the order paper at the exact hour of our ceremony. I immediately got in touch with Air Commodore Stedman who agreed to act as chairman and who, incidentally, did a very competent job. He reviewed briefly the history of aeronautical research in Canada and the organization picture as we know it. Mr Euler laid the corner-stone and was most happy in his remarks. He seemed to be greatly pleased and, I think, was genuinely touched by your specific request that he should lay the corner-stone. After Mr Euler performed this function I delivered a brief address according to the enclosed notes.

We all think of you a great deal, are very proud of the distinguished services which you are rendering, and we are confident that your responsibilities will increase as the war goes on.

As I have said before, I hesitate to bother you with long letters when I know how much concerned you are with pressing matters on the other side, but we all know how keen is your interest in this institution and we hope that you may be able to steal a few moments and find some relaxation in turning your thoughts back to the activities of the council, modest though they be in comparison to yours.

With kindest regards to Mrs McNaughton and yourself, and best wishes from the council and staff.

Sincerely yours

C.J. MACKENZIE

Ottawa
28 September 1940

Dear General McNaughton:

A great many things have happened since I last wrote to you about council business, and life has been strenuous but pleasant. Those of us who were in the last war can't help feeling that any work here is relatively unimportant compared with service overseas and there are a great many of your old friends who would like to be with you at the present time. However, there is some satisfaction in being extremely busy on work which I hope will be of some value.

In my last letter I mentioned the organization which was being formed to receive money from patriotic citizens for the purpose of supporting scientific and technical research under the National Research Council. We have received one million dollars to date and had our first meeting of the committee, which is charged with the responsibility of allocating the monies to the various projects. I was asked, particularly, to write and inform you about the meeting, give you the best wishes of the members, and tell you how much we all wished that you could be with us, as we felt you would have found great satisfaction in directing the allocation of a million dollars for special war research at the Research Council. Up to the present time the following grants have been made:

T. Eaton Company	$250,000
CPR and Consolidated Mining & Smelting Co	300,000
Bronfman Bros	250,000
International Nickel Co	250,000

These payments have all been made and it is expected that more monies will come as our work develops. The government, by Order in Council, set up a committee which is empowered to receive the monies and to allocate them to problems *selected from a list presented by the president of the National Research Council*. The direction of all researches will be handled by the council in the normal way and the committee's responsibility and authority end when they have accepted certain projects for financial support.

The committee, composed of three members of the National Research Council – Banting, Maass, and myself – J.S. Duncan, deputy minister for Air; R.A.C. Henry, member of the executive committee, Department of

Munitions and Supply; Colonel A.A. Magee, Department of National Defence; H.L. Keenleyside, Department of External Affairs; and several other government officials, held its first meeting, which was one of organization, at which I was elected chairman. The second meeting took place on September 20 and I presented a list of problems, covering the fields of chemistry, physics, engineering, medicine, etc., totalling well over a million dollars. There was no suggestion that the entire program be accepted – in fact, many of the problems have not been sufficiently worked out, but the committee did allocate $250,000 towards special projects and we are getting on with the work. There is a mission, under Sir Henry Tizard, now in America (concerning which I will say more later), and I am waiting until [Professor John] Cockcroft, Dr [G.E.G.] Bowen, Dr [Sir R.H.] Fowler, and the others get back from the USA before we will be in a position to submit details of the further work on radio which we are proposing. I only wish that you were here and could give us the benefit of your advice and experience as to some of the things which we should undertake, as I am anxious that, in connection with this fund, we spend money only on projects which are definitely of immediate military significance, and also that we get results.

My first concern is to be sure that I get able research directors. Up to the present time it has been possible to enlarge our staff by appointing junior people but, with a program double or treble the ordinary, I feel we should get some first-class senior research directors.

In chemistry, as I told you, I have appointed Dr Maass as a special assistant and he is doing first-class work. In aviation medicine, with Sir Frederick giving practically full time to the work, we have no problem. In aeronautical engineering, Parkin has a reasonably good group but we are trying to induce the British authorities to send some of their research teams to Canada for work on problems which cannot be undertaken in England, and I think that such teams could easily be integrated into Parkin's division.

The situation in physics is the most troublesome: the general administrative and professional direction is not in keeping with the high-grade personnel; the various sections are expanding rapidly and much of the new work we propose to undertake will be in the radio field. I feel the need for some first-class senior research directors and have canvassed the situation many times. Dr Fowler of Cambridge is here, as you know, in a liaison capacity, and is proving of great assistance to us. I have given him Dr Newton's office for the time being and he now feels himself almost a member of our organization. We have discussed the matter of bringing over from England some of the first-class experimentalists, either as individuals or as teams, and that may materialize. Whatever the outcome, I am quite sure one point is absolutely essential, namely, to have around us one or two top-notch senior experimental physicists.

There is on this continent now a technical and scientific mission headed by Sir Henry Tizard, whose purpose is to exchange scientific and technical information with the USA. I do not know whether you have met Sir Henry but he is an exceptionally able man whom I know you would find of interest. He is rector of the Imperial College, London, is a high-grade scientific engineer, a first-class administrator, an experienced pilot, and, as chairman of the Committee on Aeronautical Research for the past few years, has been responsible for a great deal of the organization and valuable work in that field. He brought with him on his mission Professor Cockcroft of Cambridge and Dr Bowen, who are probably two of the leading experts on RDF [radio direction finding] development in England. He also has three service officers representing the RAF, the Royal Navy, and the Army. Fowler went from here and Air Vice-Marshal Stedman, Brigadier Kenneth Stuart and I were appointed as Canadian representatives to the mission. We went to Washington and took part in the preliminary sessions. Naturally, we of the Canadian delegation could not stay more than a few days, but we made arrangements to have our technical specialists from the National Research Council and the various arms of the service go to Washington for detailed conferences on specific phases of the work. I think much good will come out of the mission and we have opened contacts for exchange of scientific information. Tizard has arranged that when he goes back to England exchanges can continue through Canadian channels.

Research Enterprises Limited, the name of the company set up by the Department of Munitions and Supply to manufacture optical glass and fire-control instruments and any other developments suggested by the National Research Council, is well under way and they have a factory being built in Toronto. Colonel W.E. Phillips of Oshawa is the president and seems to be energetic and enterprising. He has a good board of directors, including Colonel O.N. Biggar and Dr Burton. They are considering the manufacture of RDF equipment and no doubt their activities will expand.

Our staff at the council has increased materially and at the present time we have about five hundred people engaged here. The gauge laboratory has been somewhat of a problem. From a staff of two or three it has been enlarged to about fifty and the gauges are coming in at the rate of two thousand a month with the indication that before many weeks we will have to handle from six to seven thousand per month. I have had to spend a great deal of time in this laboratory as the scientific personnel are not accustomed to industrial processes and organization and, as you will well understand, a large project like this must operate more like an industrial concern. Our problem has been complicated by the fact that it has been necessary to train large numbers of people and, at the same time, attempt to turn out gauges. I found out about a week ago that there was a great lack of organization and that we were getting behind in our work. The problem of reorganization, therefore, became urgent. I have spent the major part of my time during the last four days on this problem and completed reorganization yesterday, which has been enthusiastically received by the staff and which I am sure will operate. I have divorced the strictly metrological work from the ordinary business of administration and put [Russell] Biggar from Courtice's office on records, and van Winsen, who has had considerable industrial machine-shop experience, on business management. He will be responsible to me for the efficient conduct of routine operations and for the required production.

[R.H.] Field, who has done an extraordinarily good job in accumulating and training staff, designing and procuring equipment, has been carrying an impossible load and I am going to relieve him of all routine details and keep him engaged on scientific and professional work, which he is so competent to do.

The radio laboratory has now a staff of fifty or sixty and there probably will be more expansion after Tizard and his mission have indicated some important problems which should be tackled and which they in England are not able to get on with due to restriction of flying operations.

When Tizard was in Ottawa, I arranged a meeting with Duncan and Stedman to discuss the matter of establishing experimental flying which would enable us to carry through to finality the various experimental work in de-icing, vibration, and miscellaneous aeronautical problems, aviation medical studies, radio, etc. As a result of the conference, the Department of National Defence has authorized the setting aside of four or five planes with necessary operating staff and maintenance crews and has also set up a committee consisting of Stedman, chairman, Ferrier and Bryans of the RCAF, Banting, Parkin and myself of the NRC. We consider this a useful development and are getting into operation almost immediately.

I have had many discussions with Tizard and Fowler about closer co-operation between scientific activities in England and Canada; both agree that we have resources and potentialities in Canada that are not recognized in England and are in favour of using our organization to the limit. Tizard, particularly, feels that it would be wise for England to send over several research teams which are working on problems on aeronautics, radio, etc., to carry on work here where conditions are more favourable. I told Tizard if they would send over such teams or research leaders who were top-notchers I thought we could give some financial assistance and probably take over their salaries – this to be paid from our million-dollar fund. My own feeling is that if I could get eight or ten first-class people from England who have actually been working on important problems we would be able to avoid the preliminary delays. ... My whole objective is to have all the monies at our disposal spent promptly and effectively on worth-while problems, and I have some confidence that this is being done.

With kindest regards to Mrs McNaughton and yourself, and with best wishes from the council staff.

Yours most sincerely

C.J. MACKENZIE

HQ VII Corps
Home Forces
19 October 1940

Dear Dean Mackenzie:

Long before this I should have answered your letter of 25 July 1940, written immediately after the memorable occasion in the history of the council when the foundation stone of the new laboratories was duly and properly laid. Your letter arrived in the midst of the period when we were standing guard continuously day and night against the imminent threat of the German hordes which were gathering in the ports across the narrow waters of the English Channel, and I have held it with me ever since. I have started to reply several times but in the rush of circumstances I have never been able to find words to express the deep sense of satisfaction which I feel in the fact that you and Parkin and all our other associates have been able to carry the council's plans forward to the realization that the much-needed facilities for increased research in aeronautics, optics, and the multitude of other subjects related to our war effort, will be available in time to be of help.

The kindly references which you and Mr Euler made to myself went straight to my heart and it is quite impossible to put into words how deeply I feel, but you will understand.

I am very pleased that Mr. Euler was able to be present, as in the difficult formative period, when plans were being made and conflicting interests harmonized, it was his support that alone made progress possible, and it was very fitting indeed that he should lay the foundation stone in person. Please give him my very warmest regards when you see him.

As matters stand here, with the marked improvement in the forces in the United Kingdom, their progress in re-equipment, better organization of the civil population, including the very important LDVs [local defence volunteers], and the deterioration of the weather, the menace of invasion grows less and we are able to turn our attention again to the training of our forces, to the reorganization of the units to bring into effect the most important of the lessons learned, and to the development of new methods of tactics and of new and improved equipment, all of which is most fascinating, particularly when you have, as we have in the Canadian force, a liberal endowment of men of initiative, among them experts in every conceivable branch of science and industry.

As regards innovations developed and put forward from the Canadian force, the score to date is five, which are of substantial character and which have been accepted by the British Army and are being applied generally, and I hope that we will add at least two more before Christmas.

As we had long foreseen, the scale of air attack which the Germans have been able to develop on these islands is not of a decisive order of magnitude. It is most grievous to see the beautiful old buildings and monuments in London and other cities and towns being destroyed – it is a nuisance to have factory production retarded and traffic on roads and railways delayed – it is sad to have women and children killed in raids and unpleasant that they should be forced to seek shelter underground – but none of these conditions is vital and the civilian morale is rising day by day. So we can go ahead with our plans in confidence that they can develop without hysteria and that in our own good time, when supply has caught up to our needs and when the circumstance is opportune, we will strike.

My wife has secured a small cottage near Corps Headquarters so I am living at home again. She joins me in kindest regards to you and Mrs Mackenzie and with best wishes to all at the council.

Very sincerely yours

A.G.L. McNaughton
Lieutenant-General
Commander VII Corps

Ottawa
31 October 1940

Dear General McNaughton:

Professor R.C. Wallace has handed the enclosed letter to me with the request that I have it transmitted to you. I might say that I also know Dr [A.E.] Chatwin personally as he was superintendent of the School for the Blind at Saskatoon for several years and I feel that he should be able to do well the work that he has undertaken.

Affairs are moving rapidly at the council and nearly every day something new turns up. I flew to Halifax on Tuesday and back on Wednesday and had an opportunity to see the work going on there. As you know, we have made and installed certain RDF equipment for aid in the defence system and the Navy are pleased with the results. We are at the present time working on two other projects for the Navy and doing scientific work on degaussing* and minesweeping.

As I told you in the last letter we have embarked upon a rather extensive program in radio, and at the last meeting of the War Technical and Scientific Development Committee (the committee which allocates the fund which private donors have given) we voted $370,000 for radio work for the next year and $150,000 for special investigation of wooden aircraft. We now have one and a half million dollars in the fund and there is a real disposition on the part of everyone from the ministers down to feel that scientific and technical research and developments are of the greatest importance and should be generously supported.

The British Technical Mission is in Canada now and they have been of great value to us.

Experimental flying is now organized and Banting has had some work

*Degaussing, and the supplementary process of deperming, which neutralize the magnetization of ships, were developed during the war as precautions against German magnetic mines.

carried out for him already. The Experimental Flight will consist of a squadron leader, three pilots, and the necessary ground crew. The mechanical shop at Rockcliffe will be available and at the present time we have five planes. I expect this work will develop rapidly.

Mr Davies, superintendent at Porton, arrived in Ottawa yesterday and is surveying the possible sites across Canada for field experimental work that cannot be done in England. We are expecting this phase of our activities to extend also.

The gauge laboratory is running well; we are in the happy position today of being able to calibrate about one thousand gauges a week and had an unchecked balance at the first of this week of only two hundred.

We are getting two more buildings at the annex site out of the War Technical and Scientific Development Committee's fund, one an aeronautical testing laboratory and the other an explosives testing laboratory. It is probable, as the war goes on, that we will be able to get other buildings, as needed.

We all realize how strenuous your life is and hope that you are not drawing too heavily on your reserve of health and strength. The members of the council and the staff join me in sending most cordial greetings.

With kindest personal regards to Mrs McNaughton and yourself.

Yours sincerely

C.J. MACKENZIE

HQ VII Corps
Home Forces
14 November 1940

Dear Dean Mackenzie:

This is just a line to acknowledge your letter of 31 October 1940, which has just been handed to me.

I am obliged to you for sending on the note from Dr Wallace in which he sets out the arrangements which he made with Dr Chatwin to help us with extramural studies now being organized for our men here.

Chatwin arrived yesterday and I have had a long talk with him on the subject, and I feel that we are fortunate indeed in his selection for the important work which may be done to help the men, both in their military work and, perhaps more important, in preparing them to take their places in the social, cultural, and economic life of Canada when their task with the armed forces is completed.

Your news as to the progress in the work of the council in reference to RDF, degaussing and mine-sweeping for the Navy – substantial additions to the funds at the disposal of the War Technical and Scientific Development Committee – your work with the British Technical Mission and the progress in building up an organization to carry forward experimental flying – the work on gas – the gauge laboratory and the possibilities of more buildings at the annex sites – all these are most satisfactory indeed and give one a sense of the deepest satisfaction in the way in which you and the council and its staff are serving Canada and the Empire in these critical times.

Everything goes well with us here and we are trying to take the maximum possible advantage in every way from the period of waiting, which is inevitable until supply catches up with our needs.

With kindest regards to all.

Very sincerely yours

A.G.L. McNaughton

Ottawa
6 December 1940

Dear General McNaughton:

Your cable GS 3037 regarding the development of the small air camera was received on December 1 and I immediately got in touch with Col Morrison and Dr Howlett. A telegram was despatched through Military Headquarters which I trust gave you the information required.

It is, of course, not necessary for us to assure you that we would be most anxious to undertake any further investigation or work on this or any other project that you would care to suggest to us.

I also received your letter of October 30 regarding the report which we sent to you on aircraft de-icing. The day before yesterday Mr E. Taylor of the Royal Aircraft Establishment, South Farnborough, arrived in Ottawa and I suspect that Mr Taylor's arrival and the despatch of the Blenheim for continuation of experiments in Canada resulted from your interest and influence in the matter. We feel that Mr Taylor will be useful to us as he is an extraordinarily fine type with much experience and knowledge in the entire experimental field of aeronautics, in addition to his specialty of de-icing.

The Experimental Flight has been organized and is now in operation with Wing Commander Tommy Loudon as officer in charge, and Wing Commander Halliday commanding officer of the entire establishment, including test flight, experimental flight, shops, etc. We are pleased with the organization and at the present time active work is being done on the testing of the Sperry bomb sight, on experiments in night vision which [Professor E. Godfrey] Burr of McGill has developed, and on various other projects originating in Parkin's and Banting's laboratories.

The most interesting and significant developments recently have to do with the co-operative arrangements which we have been able to make with our American friends. Sir Henry Tizard's mission which came to this country for the purpose of exchanging technical and scientific information having a war bearing with the us has had far-reaching results.

In the us there has been set up a National Defense Research Committee headed by Dr Vannevar Bush, formerly of MIT, which has initial funds amounting to ten million dollars at its disposal. The main committee is a strong one consisting of such men as President J.B. Conant of Harvard, President K.T. Compton of MIT, Dr R.C. Tolman of the University of California, Dr F.B. Jewett, chairman, Bell Laboratories, and Rear Admiral H.G. Bowen and Brigadier-General G.V. Strong, representatives of the us Navy and Army.

We have worked out an effective system for co-operation and all of the research work going on in the industrial laboratories such as those of RCA, Bell, General Electric, Westinghouse, Sperry, etc., as well as in the Navy and Army research stations, is open to representatives nominated by us, and in turn all our laboratories are open to comparable officers in the us nominated by the proper official there.

During the last few weeks we have been sending a steady stream of research men to visit laboratories in the us and in the same way we have received visits from many United States service officers and scientists. At the present time we can give to the Americans a great deal of valuable advice arising out of our year's experience of war and they thoroughly appreciate what we can do. On the other hand, they are organizing most vigorously and inside of a year we will be able to get a great deal from them.

As I told you in my last letter, the War Technical and Scientific Development Committee has already granted $370,000 for our special radio work and we will shortly have a staff of about eighty in [J.T.] Henderson's lab. The Americans are busy on similar work and the facilities of the large industrial research laboratories will be of great value to all of us. In fact we have already made arrangements whereby certain special equipment which we needed and could not have hoped to obtain for perhaps six to nine months in the normal way, will be available to us within the next six weeks at absolutely no cost to ourselves.

I have been to Washington several times to confer with Dr Bush and members of his committees there. As you well know there is a most extraordinary pro-British sentiment in such quarters. Scientifically and technically they are at war as much as we are – and one has to remind oneself continually that they are still a neutral country. Sir Frederick Banting and Colonel Gorssline, director general of Medical Services, accompanied me the last time I went down and they were able to make valuable contacts in the medical and aviation-medicine research groups. As a result of their visit, a delegation of the most prominent us scientists and service medical officers interested in aviation medicine flew to Toronto last week-end for the purpose of inspecting the work going on there and they were much impressed with what Banting and his group have done.

The work of the council is expanding day by day and new problems are flowing in continually. I have brought together in informal association Dr D.C. Rose and his group, Mr R.H. Field, Dr Archibald from [George] Laurence's laboratory, and Mr Klein from Parkin's laboratory to serve as special investigators and designers for problems suggested by Lt-Col Morrison. At the present time they are all actively working on such things as chronographs, gun sights, predictors, etc.

Parkin's laboratory is now engaged on the design of Anson wings in moulded plywood. The wind tunnel at the new annex has been held up temporarily due to the delay in obtaining the structural-steel tunnel. When we called for tenders we did not get a single bid from any firm and we had to negotiate through the Department of Munitions and Supply to have the Dominion Bridge Company instructed to take the work on. The industrial facilities of Canada are being pretty well taxed at the present time and we will soon reach the point when priorities and government instructions will have to be given for most material which has to be made in industries concerned with war work.

The work in chemistry and chemical warfare has developed rapidly and the visit of Mr Davies, superintendent of Porton, has been fruitful. I think that Davies, like all English experts who have come to Canada, has been impressed with the work and organization here, and plans have been made for the acquiring of a site fifty miles by fifty miles in Alberta* for the purpose of carrying out extensive field tests. Official negotiations have not been completed yet but when the necessary agreements have been reached, a sizeable and important work will be started.

Since the start of the war we have been able to meet the demands by increasing our junior personnel, but we are now getting to the point where we need more senior research people with experience and we are making a start on this phase. As you know I took Dr Maass on as a special assistant and have made him responsible for the administration of all extramural activities as well as the general conduct of chemical warfare work. Just recently I was able to secure the services of Dr A.G. Shenstone, professor of physics at Princeton. Shenstone has been at Princeton for a number of years but never became a naturalized American citizen, and he was anxious to return to Canada to take part in the war effort. He came at a great personal sacrifice and we are only paying him a fraction of the salary he got at Princeton. He will be useful as a liaison officer for the work going on in the US and for general consultation work in the Physics Division.

We are now negotiating for a Dr Henderson from Purdue University who is also a Canadian with a distinguished record. We have been able to obtain in a consulting capacity the services of Professor H.S. Taylor of Princeton. Taylor is head of the Chemistry Division in Princeton and one of the world's outstanding physical chemists. He is a British subject and we have appointed him as a consultant without pay to our Research Council. He will visit Ottawa from time to time and members of our staff will confer with him at Princeton as the occasion requires. As a member of our staff he also can be accredited as an official representative to visit and inspect secret work going on in the US, something which he could not have done otherwise, due to the fact that he is a British subject working in the US.

I was pleased to receive your letter of October 19 and forwarded to Senator Euler the paragraph in which you commented so kindly on his services – he was very much touched by your generous reference.

I have been writing these letters to you at monthly intervals in the way of an informal report and hope that they are of some interest to you, but if there are any aspects on which I fail to touch and on which you would like information, I hope you will let me know.

*At Suffield.

We all think of you a great deal and the various members of the staff are much interested in any news we receive and always request me to give you their very kindest regards.

My wife and I would like to send our very heartiest greetings to Mrs McNaughton and yourself with the hope that the forthcoming season may be as pleasant as possible under the trying circumstances. We are all looking forward to the day when the unpleasant task in which you are engaged will be successfully terminated and you both may return to a more intimate association with the host of friends and admirers which you have in this country.

Yours sincerely

C.J. MACKENZIE

HQ Canadian Corps
13 January 1941

Dear Dean Mackenzie:

Your letter of 6 December 1940 reached me at Canadian Corps Headquarters on 4 January 1941, and I also had one from Banting by the same mail to which I replied on 9 January, attaching a copy of a memorandum prepared for me by Rabinowitch under date of 8 January 1941. This dealt with various points raised by Banting and I am sure will give both you and him information which will be of value.

In view of the importance of this information and to guard against loss on the Atlantic, I am enclosing herewith for you a copy both of my letter to Banting and of Rabinowitch's memorandum.

Now, as regards the various points raised in your letter:

1. I was glad to have the information about the small air camera. I am sorry that this project has rested in status quo for I am sure that a small camera making use of fine-grain film and a properly designed enlarger is what is required as an answer to our very urgent problem of obtaining air photos in quantity suitable for mapping.

The whole situation in this field here is in a most unsatisfactory state, but at last the representations I have been making to the War Office, Air Ministry, Home Forces, etc., are bearing fruit and next Tuesday we are to have a comprehensive meeting to clarify the matter and to lay down a program of requirements and developments.

It is quite possible that out of this reorganization there will be opportunities for useful research and development which can be done in Canada. I propose to keep you fully informed and I feel sure that any problems which are passed to Canada will be handled with the energy and despatch for which the NRC is now well known over here.

2. I am glad that Taylor of the RAE [Royal Aircraft Establishment] has arrived and that he will be getting on with de-icing. Frankly, I am horrified at the lack of knowledge over here of past work in the field of prevention. Our reports appeared to have reached the Air Ministry but until I drew attention to them, at least some of the workers at Farnborough never seemed to have known of their existence or to have realized their value. However, that phase is over and I am sure they will rely on you more and more as Taylor's letters are received.

I can only go to the committee very rarely but if you have occasion for my intervention, do not hesitate to let me know.

3. It is most heartening to hear of the close liaison which you have developed with American science and research. The relations in and between the armies is becoming equally close and hardly a week now passes without the visit to us of distinguished, and very able American soldiers.

4. I have not been able to give much time to RDF and cognate matters but I have sent a number of our young signal officers away for special training in the new gear.

Alan Magee had talks with [Lord] Hankey, Joubert, Smith, Watson Watt and the others concerned, and Howe, Woodward, and Taylor are going into the supply problem so I think you will have the full story on their return. There has been progress to meet the night bomber but it is all most painfully slow. The whole thing needs to be tackled by fresh minds with the greatest drive that can be given and that, even now, we do not seem to get here on account of the smothering influence of bureaucracy and the never-ending series of committees with overlapping functions.

5. Glad to hear that the liaison with Morrison continues close and that Parkin's group are working on gun sights, predictors, etc.

I am up against it for an angle-of-sight instrument for use in my system of air-burst ranging which after over a quarter of a century of effort has now been adopted by the British Army. Finally, I have just been able to get a development contract given to Adam Hilger for the instrument so we may now get along with it at last.

6. I am also deep in the project with the Air Defence Command to develop new methods for producing high velocity by two novel methods. One, electrical, which Ballard knows about, and the other the conical smooth bore gun with a projectile of aerodynamic form designed to give stability at 4,000–5,000 feet per second. Parkin knows of this.

At last, after many meetings with committees, I am to discuss the project tomorrow with senior officials in the Ministry of Supply and we may get something going. If we are to beat the night bomber we must cut the time of flight to 25,000 feet to 10 seconds or less which means a MV of perhaps 6,000 foot seconds.

7. The work in chemical-warfare defence is fully commented on in Rabinowitch's letter, which is very informative. He has his mobile laboratory in great shape, the envy of other corps, and with him on guard I feel that we will know at once what to do to protect our men against any CW threat the enemy may use.

As you have no doubt heard, VII Corps became Canadian Corps on Christmas Day and I am now busy changing our staff and rearranging the organization. It all is going well if somewhat slowly and I hope before spring to have everything thoroughly balanced and efficient. We must patiently wait for Canadian industry to supply many of the weapons of which we are in need and I pray that battle may not come to us till we have been completed.

My wife is well and we often speak of you all at the National Research Council. I wish you were nearer so that we could lean more heavily on you for the solution of the many research problems which face us daily.

My wife joins me in kindest regards to you and Mrs Mackenzie and all at the council.

Very sincerely yours

A.G.L. McNaughton
Lieutenant-General
Commander Canadian Corps

Ottawa
11 February 1941

Dear General McNaughton:

Sir Frederick Banting has just come into my office and told me that he is leaving for England tomorrow by bomber plane, and I am dashing off this note which he has agreed to take.* Banting has been feeling for some time that someone should go to England and get first-hand information concerning medical problems. Dr Best has been wanting to go and we finally made arrangements but he then decided he had other work to do so Banting is going. He is bucked up about the prospects of flying.

I received your letter of 13 January yesterday and was very glad to hear from you. We all join with you in the wish that we were nearer so that we could be of more direct assistance and have the advantage of your drive and initiative.

Affairs here seem to move in cycles. At times we seem to be making excellent progress; at other times we seem to get bogged down by bureaucratic machinery and have a feeling that we are in a treadmill without getting anywhere. However, things are moving and I suppose our moments of depression are due to the fact that we all want to do so much more than seems possible to achieve.

We have worked out an excellent liaison with the Navy. They have appointed us their official research station and Rose is the liaison officer at the Research Council for naval problems. They have appointed Lt-Commander Millard to be the naval technical liaison officer and many problems are under way.

Dr George S. Field left for England on Sunday to get first-hand information on a number of problems which we understand are breaking, and we are rapidly building up a section to deal with the various problems in anti-submarine and minefields. Field was down to Washington recently and got much valuable information. One of the most depressing things about the Admiralty is that Wright absolutely refuses to deal with the Research Council as such. He will write to Boyle or [George] Henderson of Halifax or any other individual that he wants to, but he will not write officially to this office. It borders on insolence and, if there were not a war on, I would raise an issue as he writes to these people and asks them for favours which involve financial commitments of the council. Naturally we

*This is the letter Sir Frederick Banting had with him when he met his death, 21 February 1941.

cannot afford to let anything interfere with possible contributions to the cause, but it is annoying. The Air Ministry is not much better but Gough and the Ministry of Supply are absolutely first class and the co-operation and communication with that ministry leave nothing to be desired.

Burr of McGill has made what may prove to be one of the most valuable scientific contributions that Canada will make. The Navy people, after seeing a demonstration of his ideas, were most enthusiastic and wanted Burr to go to England immediately to demonstrate it to the Admiralty. However, as George Field was going anyway, I thought it would be a waste of time for Burr to spend a couple of months for a few hours' demonstration, and in addition I was anxious that [George] Field get a good entrée to Admiralty circles. Field or Banting will tell you what the idea is as I don't want to put it on paper. It is one of those things which would be of great value to the Germans and if it can be kept perfectly secret it may prove a powerful aid for naval purposes.*

The magnesium pot is boiling again. I fear that when the story is told of magnesium it may not be an attractive one, for as far as we can see there seems to be a concerted effort on the part of the interests in England to prevent any developments in Canada. You probably know that there have been many negotiations carried on between the Aluminium Company and Magnesium Electron and between other bodies. Blaylock of the Consolidated Mining and Smelting Co was interested in a way in one phase of it and Noranda has also shown some interest.

[L.M.] Pidgeon's work has completely justified the plans which you laid. He is now recognized as the best independent expert in the magnesium field in Canada and has even been called in by parties in the United States. At the present time a group of Canadian people headed by Jowsey and Segsworth, with excellent backing by most of the first-class mining men, have raised $150,000 to put Pidgeon's development through the pilot-plant stage, and I think there may be some interesting developments come out of that.

I have seen the Honourable Messrs Ralston and Howe, Major-General [H.D.G.] Crerar and Colonel Magee since their return and have first-hand information about your activities and achievements in England. Ralph Bell gave a dinner at the country club last Saturday night for

---

*Professor E. Godfrey Burr had devised a method of camouflaging ships at night (when they appear as blackened objects against a lighter background) by means of automatic diffused floodlighting. His scheme had just been tested for the first time on 22 January 1941.

Ralston and Howe and they both gave informative, intimate stories of their experiences, all of which was interesting.

There has been another change in the office of the deputy minister of Air, Mr J.S. Duncan retiring and Mr DeCarteret of Montreal taking over. Duncan was an able and competent man and was a great friend of the Research Council. We are all sorry to see him go.

Our work in aeronautical engineering is not developing as well as we thought. Parkin has an excellent staff of about twenty keen, alert young men but no work for them. We thought that when the experimental-flight organization was set up we would have lots of work but someway or other it has got absorbed in army routine and at the present time is nothing more than a glorified test flight with reports being made out by junior officers of the Air Force on matters in which we have specialized for many years. We have competent workers but few references come to us. There seems to be a complete lack of any co-operation between research stations in England and here, and we are much disturbed about the matter. I have come to the conclusion that the only way to get things moving is to send two of our men to England, and we are now negotiating for a trip by Green and [M.S.] Kuhring of Parkin's division.

We have been interested in developing wooden aircraft and have made up miscellaneous parts and are studying the scientific and technical design aspects in this new medium, but it seems absolutely impossible to get in action. Everyone appears to assume that we should be canvassing this matter seriously but we are blocked when it comes to getting any authority to design and construct an aeroplane in the moulded wooden plastic construction. I am afraid that the whole aeroplane situation in Canada is not so attractive a picture as the rest of the munitions program.

Our liaison with the Army and the Ministry of Supply in England is excellent. The Chemical Warfare Section is coming on well and all the work in RDF is being carried on with the greatest efficiency, despatch and co-operation.

I was down in Hamilton last week and saw the first shipment of 3.7 guns turned out by the Westinghouse Company. The Otis-Fensom people are also making guns and as far as I can see they are doing the work extraordinarily well. Incidentally, the annual meeting of the Engineering Institute of Canada was held at Hamilton and the award to you of the Kennedy medal was received with the greatest applause and enthusiasm. As president of the Engineering Institute for this year I was instructed to send the best wishes of the institute to you and Mrs MacNaughton for the coming year.

Colonel [F.C.] Wallace, who came over as one of the service officers with Sir Henry Tizard's mission, was retained in Canada by the general staff for general instructional purposes, as he was in charge of anti-aircraft batteries and was one of the senior officers who went through the whole Dunkirk show. He is an extremely able officer, a fine gentleman, and scientifically and technically well equipped. I saw Major-General Crerar and Brig Stuart last week and suggested to them that Wallace be appointed to the council as liaison officer by the services. This they agreed to and the system is working out well as Wallace is persona grata in all the military and naval circles in the United States as well as in Canada. He is a great friend of Brig Letson, Canadian military attaché in Washington, and his appointment will facilitate visits of our people to the military and naval stations in the States, the acquisition of information, and general co-ordination.

The Governor General has been around to visit us three times in the last few months and while I don't think his knowledge is as extensive or his detailed interest as keen as those of Lord Tweedsmuir, he is interested in our work and we have enjoyed his visits greatly.

One interesting development concerns the protection of scientific war workers in outside laboratories. As you probably know, we have fifty or sixty people working in the various university laboratories on dangerous war work with poison gases, explosives, and aviation. Up to the present these people have absolutely no protection in case of accident or harm from enemy action on the seas or on land. I had the matter investigated and decided that we have precedent for having these people covered under the regulations of the Department of Pensions. I had an Order in Council prepared and submitted through the Honourable Mr MacKinnon, and the War Council kindly endorsed the proposition. We are expecting that it will go through any day now.

I attended the annual banquet of the executive officers of the Pulp and Paper Association in Montreal last week and was asked to speak. Everyone that I met wanted to be remembered to you and all the people connected with forestry appreciate the work which you have done in that field.

I was going to have the book which you requested on projecting of shells by electricity taken by Banting in the plane but, as the weight of the luggage which he can take is reduced to a minimum, I sent it by Dr Field instead.

Banting will be able to tell you anything else about the council which you may be interested in and I am spending this evening with him when we will go over possible items of interest.

My wife joins me in sending the kindest regards to both you and Mrs MacNaughton and the very best luck for the coming year. While we all realize that your services in England at the present time are of the greatest importance we, nevertheless, wish many times that you could be in Canada to give leadership and forcefulness where needed.

With kindest regards, I am,

Sincerely yours

C.J. MACKENZIE

Ottawa
5 March 1941

Dear General McNaughton:

I have just returned from Sir Frederick's funeral. He was buried in Toronto on Tuesday afternoon, March 4. You will appreciate more than anyone else how much his loss means to the Research Council and particularly to me at the present time, as he has been a tower of strength and a warm personal friend throughout the months.

Ever since he returned last year he has been anxious to get back to England, but both Brigadier Gorssline, DMC [Director, Medical Corps of Canada] and I felt that he was so vital in the organization here, which was developing rapidly, that we should hold him in Canada. However, a few weeks ago when things began to look bad in England he insisted he must go over and see for himself what the conditions were, take information from Canada to England, and bring back to Canada problems which we might undertake. His interest in aviation, coupled with his desire to get to England as quickly as possible, was responsible for his making the trip by plane. It is a great tragedy that, of all the planes flown over, the one carrying Banting is the only one that has been lost.

The plane left Newfoundland on Thursday night, February 20, and was heard from by radio about forty-five minutes after the take-off, but never again. Air Commodore Cuffe, RCAF, telephoned me Friday about three P.M. and told me that he had very bad news, that Sir Frederick's plane was overdue and in all probability was lost, but that no public announcement would be made for a few days. I went down to Toronto Saturday to see Lady Banting and she was bearing up well. She has been courageous throughout the whole show and is behaving in the way that he would have wished.

On Monday I was in a meeting when a radio flash came through stating that the plane had been sighted and that there were signs of life. I was sure in my own mind that Sir Frederick was alive and rushed out to telephone Air Vice-Marshal [L.D.D.] McKean, the RAF liasion officer in Ottawa, who told me that he had just got the latest flash, that the plane had been sighted and there was writing on the snow to the effect that the pilot was alive and the other three dead. This was the hardest blow to take after having our hopes revived. They were not able to get the bodies out for nearly a week, as the flying weather was bad.

The bodies were flown to Toronto and the funeral held in Convocation Hall, under the joint control of the university and the military authorities. It was a large and impressive ceremony, as you would realize. Canon Cody, president of the University of Toronto, preached a sermon and did it well. I represented the Research Council as one of the chief mourners, and Parkin, Maass, Collip, and [Dr Wynn] Billingsley also came down.

The papers across Canada, of course, paid magnificent tribute to Banting and I think that perhaps for the first time the general public realized that Banting was even greater the last few years than during the insulin period, and that his modesty, simplicity, and real greatness probably were brought to light through his work on the Research Council and the Associate Committees on Medical and Aviation Medical Research. Those of us who know the part which you played in bringing Banting on the council, and particularly in making him assume the chairmanship of the Associate Committee of Medicine, fully appreciate what you did for Banting, for the Research Council, and for the country. He has told me many times that the happiest period of his life has been the period in which he was associated with the council and, as you know, he had an admiration and an affection for you which was, I think, a great compliment to both.

Banting did not leave on the plane in any sense of adventure. He did not go to England for personal reasons. In fact, if he had consulted his own considerations, which he never did, he would have stayed here, absorbed in the work he was doing, and he would not have attempted to fly the Atlantic. He did both because of a stern sense of duty and because in times of war he was really, at heart, first a soldier. He knew that you would like to see him in England. He felt that the times were critical and that he should be there. He felt that, as he was head of aviation research, he should have all the experiences that the pilot and airman had. We mourn the result, but the decision was true to form and, if he had not so decided, he would not have been the personality that we all loved and respected.

The details of the accident are not out at the present time. Air Commodore Edwards and two other air officers are now in Newfoundland investigating. The details that have come out make a strange picture. There were apparently five planes in the party leaving Newfoundland. The other four arrived in England safely. The one got out over the Atlantic a few miles when one engine cut off. The pilot apparently asked for a bearing and started back. The second engine cut off and he made a forced landing. There have been contradictory reports that he told the others to bail out but they did not do so; that Banting bailed out at too low an altitude (which apparently is not true); that the plane landed safely and was only damaged when one of the landing wheels gave way and it swung around on the ice and crashed into trees, etc. The only thing that is clear to date is that the pilot was not badly hurt and that the other three were killed, which, I think you will admit, is a most unusual type of accident. Apparently the navigator and radio man were killed instantaneously. The meagre reports indicate that Banting lived from six to twenty-four hours. I had a talk with the doctor who performed the post-mortem in Toronto and he said that the injuries were such that there is little likelihood that he would have recovered had he been placed in a first-class hospital and under expert professional skill. We will know the details later on, but at the present time the pilot is in hospital in Montreal and has given no official testimony as far as I know. I should think that after the investigation the situation will be clarified.

I have been somewhat concerned about the estate, as Sir Frederick had told me, the last time he went overseas, that he went in uniform in order to get protection for his wife and family as his total estate would be insignificant. After his death I immediately got in touch with Mr J.S. Duncan, who until recently, as you know, was acting deputy minister for Air but is now back in Toronto as president of the Massey-Harris Co. Duncan is an extraordinarily fine businessman. Through the Research Council he made many contacts with Banting and was very fond of him. Duncan and I got a conference with the executor last Monday and things were much as I had anticipated. He had some insurance which may be invalidated by the circumstances, but Duncan immediately got in touch with Sir Edward Beatty and Morris Wilson by telephone and I think they may be able to establish a case. The matter hinges on whether or not Banting was paying his fare. I stated that the Research Council had given the British government five thousand dollars' worth of special equipment and that Banting himself had given medical supplies, vaccines, etc., which the British government needed, and in view of these and other tangible considerations, the company agreed to carry him. If they cannot make this stick, we will have to try something else because up to the present time, after meeting obligations, there is practically nothing.

As a result of the tragedy I have a number of difficult problems on my shoulders. Banting was in the army but head of aviation medical research and, as you know, there is now an RCAF medical service. Banting also had his laboratory in Toronto working almost exclusively on medical problems and there is no successor in sight for either one of these problems. I can have Collip take over the chairmanship of the Associate Committee on Medical Research, but the other two cases require careful handling as there are many cross currents and personalities involved and much danger that his organization will dissolve into ineffectiveness. I had a talk with President Cody of the University of Toronto on Tuesday and another with Group Captain Ryan and I have worked out a plan which, if it goes through, will, I think, allow us to carry on effectively. Strange as it may seem, at the present time I am practically obliged to carry the administrative direction of all the medical work. Colonel Duncan Graham, who is a professor of medicine at Toronto and also a special consultant to Brigadier Gorssline, DMC, is a great friend of the council's, and Collip has been developing rapidly, so that my personal relations with the various medical groups are good, but some permanent basis will have to be reached before we can feel happy about the situation.

The work of the council is increasing day by day and the pressure at times has been great. The week that Banting died it looked as if my staff were vanishing. Eagleson has been ordered away for a month due to ill health; Maass, who has been carrying a terrific load and has been of the greatest assistance to me, is on the verge of a nervous collapse and I cannot get him away for a rest; Flood, whom I think is today the greatest expert in chemical warfare on the American continent, has been working very hard with a resultant breakdown and we will have to send him away for two weeks. However, we will have to carry on.

Langmuir of General Electric was up here over a week ago and spent the day with Flood. Langmuir has been attacking the problem of smoke penetration of gas masks from a fundamental point of view and had conceived certain fundamental theories. He came to Ottawa, spent a day with Flood, and went back much impressed with the work that was going on here. Although he had to modify his theories completely, he was most delighted with his experience and said he would return for more consultation with our staff. He had, incidentally, spent two days of the previous week with one of the largest chemical-warfare institutions in the United States and he told Professor Taylor of Princeton (who is a Britisher), that his visit there was a waste of time and that our fundamental work was far ahead of theirs.

Professor Fowler will be returning to England shortly and his place will be taken by Sir Lawrence Bragg, who is Rutherford's successor in the Cavendish Laboratory, Cambridge. [Sir Charles] Darwin of NPL is also coming to this continent and will be stationed at Washington, so that we will have here two of Britain's leading physicists.

The political pot in Canada is boiling a bit and the Department of Munitions and Supply has been having a rough passage in the House. I think there is no suggestion of any scandal and it seems to me that the situation is not unexpected; even under the best conditions, deliveries and performance are always behind promises and expectations. Howe is a great fighter, however, and I think temporarily is on top again.

We have had messages from Dr Green and Dr [George] Field, who have apparently seen you, and Parkin will see that you get the progress reports on the auto sights as requested.

I don't know whether copies of Banting's reports have been coming by alternative routes, but I gave instructions some time ago that all important documents should be sent by alternative routes and I will ask Dr Billingsley, secretary of the Medical Committee, to check this matter.

We have been working on the development of a very rugged radio tube which can be inserted in a shell and take $36000g$ and stand also the necessary centrifugal forces. Such a tube has been developed and is being put into production, and is awaiting only the development of the radio devices to complete the proximity fuse. Cockcroft of the Ministry of Supply knows all about this development.

As I have said before, we all wish that the Research Council were closer to you and could be of greater personal service, and it is unnecessary for me to tell you that any problem which you have in mind will be tackled by our staff with the greatest enthusiasm and interest.

I am sending a copy of this letter by alternative routes.

With the kindest regards to Mrs McNaughton and yourself from all your many friends in the council,

Sincerely yours

C.J. MACKENZIE

HQ Canadian corps
9 April 1941

Dear Dean Mackenzie:

This morning I have your letter of 14 March with which was enclosed:

1. A copy of Dr Howlett's memorandum entitled, "On Aerial Survey Photography and Allied Work Carried out under the Associate Committee on Survey Research."

2. A copy of Mr R.H. Field's memorandum entitled, "Instruments Designed for the Associate Committee of Survey Research," dated 21 February 1941.

Also the photographs and blueprints referred to in the above.

I am afraid the originals of these reports, which you advise were despatched by diplomatic bag on 26 February 1941, must have been lost at sea for they have never arrived at Canadian Corps.

These reports will be very useful to us in the survey work we are now undertaking and I will also see that the information is given to the Air Ministry War Office Committee on Air Survey Development.

We look forward to having the three small precision survey cameras promised in your cable GS 1708, dated 25 March 1941.

With kindest regards to all and many thanks for your help in this matter,

Very sincerely yours

A.G.L. McNaughton

Ottawa
11 April 1941

Dear General McNaughton:

We have received several letters and cables from you recently on specific matters and have answered them as promptly as possible, but I am writing this as a general, informal news-letter.

1. I thought you might be interested in a list of some of the research projects which we have under way and I am accordingly enclosing two lists, one of the work being done under the special war appropriation to the council and the other of the projects being carried on under the War Technical and Scientific Development Committee trust fund (I also attach hereto a list of the donors to this fund).

You will see that the ordinary list includes those projects which are now concerned particularly with the production of gear and prototypes; all these projects are receiving considerable attention. Under the War Technical and Scientific Development Committee fund we are supporting researches in university labs, which you will note under C1000 and P1000, and there are twenty different projects under way at the present time at the universities.

ME1002 – Aeronautical Engineering – is to take care of a special building for structural tests of aircraft, which has already been erected at the new site on the Montreal Road.

You will notice that the grant for radio (P1003) is the largest and I am sure you will be pleased to hear that we have already made several prototypes which are going into production and will be in active-service use soon.

In addition to the formal list we, of course, undertake many smaller projects from day to day.

2. Our finances at the present time are quite satisfactory. The normal vote has not been cut appreciably and, with the War Technical and Scientific Development Committee fund, the various funds made available by other departments for special work, and the expenditures on the new buildings, we will have been responsible for the spending of from five to six million dollars for this year.

3. The buildings on the Montreal Road are about ready and Parkin plans to move out there in a couple of weeks. The architectural treatment has been quite successful and I think you will be satisfied with the layout. The General Administration Building is attractive and your office will make a pleasant retreat in the years to come.

The main delay has been in the steel work for the wind tunnel. When we called for tenders no company submitted any, and we had to have the work ordered done through the Department of Munitions and Supply. However, everything is proceeding well at the present time.

4. We are in the midst of organizing the Associate Committee on Aviation

Medicine. As you know, Sir Frederick carried the load in this field and there is no one who can really fill his place. In all probability Colonel Duncan Graham, who has been vice-chairman, will take over the chairmanship and we are hoping that arrangements may be made at Toronto University whereby Banting's lab will continue to devote its energies to aviation medicine until the end of the war.

5. Lady Banting came to Ottawa a couple of weeks ago and spent the week-end with us. She brought with her a manuscript on the story of insulin which Sir Frederick wrote in England in the winter of 1940 when he had some leisure time. There was only one copy in existence so Miss [Doreen] Geary typed the whole thing out from dictation by Lady Banting.

It is a remarkable document and written extraordinarily well. I have seen a lot of his memoranda, etc., but never realized that he had literary talents. Some bits from the insulin story and also some of the passages from other diary notes which Lady Banting brought with her, will, I think, make literary gems which will live for all time.

Sir Frederick made a habit over the past twenty years of writing notes and diary entries every day. He put down his innermost thoughts and a great many of the sketches are excellent. In one of his diaries he has written an appreciation of you which is very fine and shows both insight and true appreciation of worth. I suggested to Lady Banting that she should have this bit copied out and sent to you directly before anything is done about formal publication.

We have discussed the matter of publication of the insulin story and diaries and I think that if a first-rate man could have the material he could make a small book of these autobiographical notes which would have universal appeal and show the development of a great man and the trials and tribulations through which a great soul passed.

Banting was a simple man in many ways but his character was also very complex. He had many facets and an amazing number of talents which he developed by sheer persistence – research, painting, writing, wood carving, methodical reading of literature and history. All these things he set his mind to and succeeded in.

A complete biography of Banting can, of course, not be written now. There was too much heat and passion in his life twenty years ago and many of the actors of that period are still alive. Many of those whom he despised and hated twenty years ago have become his closest, most intimate and loyal friends today and some of those who were closest to him then became incompatible throughout the years. It would be unwise to open up all the old controversial issues, but some day his complete life with all its strengths and all its weaknesses should be written for posterity.

6. March was a busy month as we had our council meeting and also a meeting of the War Technical and Scientific Development Committee – both in the last two weeks – and there were many problems before both bodies.

7. Research Enterprises is getting on well and they have a most creditable plant in operation in Toronto. The president, Colonel Phillips, DSO, MC, is an efficient businessman and has done a marvellous job.

They have already made optical glass and are in production on fire-control instruments. The radio building is practically completed and they are working in sections of it now. From the time the plans were laid until they started manufacturing optical instruments, only a little over six months elapsed and within nine months from the time of starting they will be in commercial production of optical glass.

8. We have entered into an arrangement with a group of mining interests to put Pidgeon's method of production of magnesium by the thermal process through the pilot-plant stage. A group of interested and wealthy mining men formed a company and raised $160,000 to do the work and we made an agreement whereby they would stand all of the actual cost and pay us overhead; if the work is successful and the process is used commercially, they will pay us thirty thousand dollars cash.

9. The gauge laboratory is going along reasonably well although the exact relationship between the gauge lab, the Department of Munitions and Supply and the Inspection Board has never been clearly defined, and the demand has never caught up with our facilities.

There has been formed an Inspection Board of the United Kingdom and Canada with Major-General R.F. Lock as chairman and Colonel K.S. Maclachlan, Colonel G.B. Howard, and Colonel Victor Sifton as members of the board. This board is to undertake responsibility for the financing of the gauge laboratory and I think they are to appoint a representative on the Inspection Board who will be responsible for all negotiations on tolerances, acceptances, etc.

I am going to divorce the main gauge laboratory from the Metrology Section as the laboratory is really an industrial-engineering type of activity and not a scientific laboratory in the ordinary sense. We will use the Metrology Section as a consultant service for all of the laboratories.

10. The work in chemical warfare is developing well. Plans have been completed for the purchase of a large tract of land in Alberta about twenty to thirty miles square on which field tests will be carried out. It is estimated that expenditures this year will amount to somewhere between one and a half to two million dollars.

Mr Davies, superintendent of Porton, is here now and will be able to see that the work is directed in the proper way.

It is not quite clear to date whether the expenditure will be made under the Defence Department or under Munitions and Supply, but at any rate there will probably be a director of Chemical Warfare who will represent the appropriate government department and be responsible for general administrative matters. The technical and scientific direction will be under the control of a committee of the Research Council and the Defence Department. Actually, the Research Council will be the essential director of this project.

11. The work on research for the Navy is progressing well. As Navy matters are assuming a greater importance daily in the Dominion, this phase of our work will grow. In order to make for more effective liaison with the Admiralty, the Navy has formally made the National Research Council its scientific research station and has named the president of the National Research Council as the director of Scientific Research. Dr D.C. Rose is the deputy DSR and is responsible for general oversight of the naval-research work.

We have a considerable number of problems under way in connection with the Navy, and that service has put two hundred thousand dollars into its estimates this year to be spent on research work under our direction.

12. Mr A.H.R. Smith of the Radio Section, who was proceeding to England to replace [D.W.R.] McKinley, just returned to Ottawa after having spent nearly a month on the high seas. His boat started off in convoy but had three serious accidents during the journey, which makes one suspicious of sabotage. After being completely disabled for some time in one of the danger zones it finally made its way back to New York. Smith is waiting to start off again and it is hoped that he may be able to get over by air this time.

13. During the last month I have had some interesting discussions with Mr Howe, Mr Harry Carmichael of the Department of Munitions and Supply and Colonel Victor Sifton, acting MGO. As you undoubtedly know, there has been going on a reorganization of the MGO branch at Ottawa and

many methods of handling technical and engineering design, etc., have been canvassed. I was approached to take over the task of organizing and assuming responsibility for all design and engineering aspects for the Department of Munitions and Supply, but naturally could not assume this responsibility without giving up my present position which, of course, is unthinkable. However, the suggestion is a compliment to the work the council has done over the years and the Department of Munitions and Supply have recognized our function and are proposing to name us as their official scientific research station just as the Navy has done.

14. There is one matter on which I would like to have your opinion if you have time to consider it at all. As you know, Dr Newton has been occupying the position of dean of Agriculture at the University of Alberta for the past year. When he decided to leave the council, I asked him to withdraw his resignation as I would prefer to grant him a year's leave of absence. There were two reasons for doing this: I had hoped that he might change his mind and decide to remain in Ottawa, and I was not anxious to assume the responsibility of appointing a successor.

Newton was here a few weeks ago and at that time he felt that he would probably stay in Alberta, so that his resignation from the council would come into effect soon. Naturally, I am not prepared to make any permanent appointment in his place while you are away, but I think in the interests of efficient operation it will be necessary to appoint an acting director.

After considering the matter carefully and observing different people, I feel that Dr W.H. Cook is probably the ablest man whom it would be possible to get for this position. It is true that he is comparatively young but he is as mature as Dr Steacie, if not more so, and he is not only extraordinarily able intellectually, but he is a good administrator and easy to work with.

I invited him into the last council meeting to report on what was being done in connection with secondary uses for agricultural products in Canada, and without any notice at all, he gave a clear presentation of a difficult subject and all the members of council were much impressed. My proposal, if it meets with your approval, would be to appoint [Dr W.H.] Cook as acting director until you return, but fix his salary at the level of research biologist only, so that if a different final selection for director were made, he could still remain at the salary rank of his acting-director status, which would not be out of line with his capabilities and responsibilities.

15. We are having some difficulties with our subprofessional staff, particularly in the Radio Section where we have sixty men classified as lab helpers and assistants although they are really electricians and machinists working on the development of radio apparatus. Their pay is much below that which they can get in industry or in the services, and the regulations of the Treasury Board make it almost impossible to get a satisfactory settlement. I am considering having all the subprofessionals in the Radio Section carried on the staff of Research Enterprises Limited, for whom, of course, we are making the prototypes. At the present time I can see no objection to this procedure, as by this means we would get the desired results without interfering with the normal council staff.

This whole subprofessional problem is a great one, as there is a heavy demand from industry and the services for this category, namely the bright young graduates of technical schools who are mechanically inclined and who, within a few months, become quite expert at mechanical and technical procedures.

16. Sir Lawrence Bragg and Dr Charles Darwin arrived in Ottawa last Wednesday and stayed until Sunday night. I gave Bragg your cable and he was much interested. I had already discussed the request contained in the cable with Parkin and he is having his staff study the matter to see what we can do. As soon as Bragg returns from Washington we will go into the matter more thoroughly.

We enjoyed Darwin's visit. He is a most enjoyable and interesting person and I think should do quite well in the us where he will be at the head of the Central Scientific Office of the British Purchasing Commission. Bragg went to Washington with Darwin on Sunday to familiarize himself with the entire North American picture before returning to Ottawa.

I think Bragg will fit in well here. He is perhaps quieter than Darwin and less aggressive than Fowler, but is a sound physicist and should be a great help to us.

17. I don't think I ever told you that Mrs Sharp resigned in January in order to start life all over again. She expects to become a mother for the seventh time, I believe, within the next month or so and consequently found it impossible to carry on here. I think she is pleased over the whole affair.

The news of the last few days has not been cheering but I suppose reverses are to be expected and we are all hoping that the next few months will bring greater things for us. We all think of you a great deal and you have the best wishes of the whole council behind you at all times.

My wife joins me in sending very best regards to you and Mrs McNaughton.

Sincerely yours

C.J. MACKENZIE

Ottawa
19 June 1941

Dear General McNaughton:

It is almost two months since I have written to you my 'monthly newsletter' but time flies by rapidly and we seem to be getting busier all the time.

I received your letter of May 19 with the enclosed copy of Twyman's book on spectro-chemical analysis and will see that Drs Laurence and Howlett have an opportunity of looking it over. I also received your letter of March 21 in which you expressed appreciation that we have been able to maintain our grants for post-graduate research workers. I have shown this to several of the university presidents who have been much heartened in their work to know that you, who are so closely in contact with the serious business of war, should feel that graduate work is still important.

It is interesting to see the way the work of the council develops from day to day and how the emphasis shifts. One thing which pleases me is the realistic view which all the members of the staff here take. We all feel keenly that unless our endeavours produce equipment and findings of use to the man in the field we will not be achieving our fundamental purpose, for we all realize that, in modern warfare based on science, technology, and mass production, there are three stages – research and development, production, and use in the field. In the first year and a half, work here was entirely on research and development and, of course, that work is still going on, but we are getting to the production field now, and particularly in the radio field the boys are working night and day to get out prototypes of equipment which is going into operation.

I feel that the next phase, particularly on the complicated equipment, will be operation, and I can see the time when a large number of specialists will be used directly in the operation of the equipment we are producing and in the chemical-warfare field or in instruction work in close co-operation with the services.

When the gauge laboratory was organized I insisted that so far as possible women be used, and at a recent meeting of directors we decided that, as far as possible, we would gradually replace the young, physically fit subprofessionals of military age by girls, and we now have in our employ fifty or sixty. Just the other day the Honourable Mr Ralston made a public appeal to the departments in Ottawa to follow this policy and we were in the enviable position of having anticipated the situation.

Our RDF work is going on splendidly. We have manufactured a prototype for GL [gun-laying radar equipment] which is ready to go into operation, and you will be pleased to know that Research Enterprises Limited has now received an order for twenty-six million dollars' worth of this equipment to be supplied to Britain under the lend-lease bill, this in spite of the fact that many of the people in England have been telling us ever since the start of the war that we could not develop or manufacture such things in Canada. We have been doing a great deal of work for the Navy who are now highly enthusiastic about RDF applications. We have land stations in operation in Halifax and have already equipped three or four corvettes and destroyers of the RCN; last week we actually put a set on one of the RN battleships and have immediately received orders for twenty more.

The ASV [air-to-surface vessels] equipment is now in production and we feel that the results obtained in RDF alone have already justified all of the expenditures made by the Research Council to date. Every day new problems are arising and every day the services become more interested.

The RDF work is peculiar in the sense that all of the services are interested and the work must be co-ordinated. In this regard the Chiefs of Staff decided to set up a committee to have complete charge of all RDF work. On the committee there are representatives from the operational and technical branches of the Army, Navy, and Air Force, Research Enterprises and the National Research Council. I was asked to assume the chairmanship of this committee and agreed on the understanding that the committee would have real authority and could not be blocked by minor officers. This was agreed to and now, in the case of any dispute as between the three services in the matter of standardization of fundamental units, I have access to the Chiefs of Staff committee and indirectly to the ministers. At the present time the work seems to be going smoothly.

Howlett is doing a lot of valuable work. He trained a group to manufacture quartz discs for Asdics and the actual production work is now being done in the Department of Mines. Before turning over the work the group was producing ninety-two per month and the full-scale production required is 100–150, so that he really turned over a going concern. He is also working on twenty-five anti-aircraft directors for Munitions and Supply and a number of smaller instruments. We are building range finders, instruments to calibrate fortress position finders, and doing work on night photography, small air cameras, etc.

Rose's work with the Navy is developing rapidly. They are most enthusiastic and the co-operation is ideal. In fact, they have officially recognized the Research Council as their research station in the Navy List.

Ballard is designing all magnetic sweeps and the group at Halifax on degaussing and deperming is developing rapidly; we will probably have a group of fifty or sixty there shortly.

Rose is developing a flash spotting computer for firing guns and this project is getting along reasonably well.

In aviation medicine there is a great deal of useful work being done but the liaison with England is not as good as it should be. For your confidential ears there is a feeling here that Whittingham still feels that nothing good can come out of Canada or the United States, and whether this is true or not it tends to take the heart out of some of the work.

In biology, [Dr W.H.] Cook has just made what seems to be an extraordinarily ingenious and valuable development. There is a great dearth of refrigerating space on boats and a great demand for bacon. There was an urgent call for shipments of bacon in temporary refrigeration and Cook worked out an idea of placing bacon beneath the water line in boats and circulating cold air from mechanical refrigerating units around the cargo. There were a lot of restrictions and the use of insulating material was not allowable due to the fact that it would crush and shift the cargo. Cook made all the designs, got the special refrigerating units built, installed them on the boat and has a man on the boat for England – all within a short space of time. If the experiment is successful it will be a useful bit of work.

In aeronautical engineering we are proceeding actively with the construction of aircraft in moulded plywood construction and have made various integral parts for the Air Ministry. We are also testing full-scale models of wings and fuselages made in the same material.

Klein and his group are working full time on design and the shop is actually producing predictors, gun sights, etc., for coast defences.

The de-icing experiments are bogging down a bit and, again for your private information, the co-operation with the Air Force is not so good as with the other services. I don't think there is any disposition on the part of anyone to disapprove of scientific and technical work but the air staff are not scientifically minded and, quite naturally perhaps, are inclined to concentrate on training and ordinary affairs. The result is that personnel are taken away from the testing and development flight, and there is also a tendency for the Air Force to hire young technical people (who would be very junior on our staff) and have them undertake their own technical work, which our people are much more competent to do. This may be only a passing phase but it is disturbing and, we feel, may curtail the amount of useful work which we can do in aeronautical research. On the de-icing work, the British sent one of their experts to Canada and he is so discouraged with the co-operation that he threatens to return to England. However, this is perhaps over-emphasizing a minor point and is not caused by any unfriendliness to us as an institution or personally by any of the staff. It probably is due to the fact that, while in Canada the Navy and the Army are interested in operations and are much aware of the value of technical and scientific things, the complete problem of the Air Force to date has been training.

Another new development within the last month is the organization of a section of cryptanalysis. The various departments – External Affairs, Navy, Army, Air Force, RCMP – all had an interest but did not know how to organize. The National Research Council put up ten thousand dollars, brought in some experts and are giving the thing a six months' trial. If the section is successful in decoding a substantial number of messages, the government will then organize a regular service to take over.

Dr George Field returned from the Old Country and had one of the most interesting experiences that I think any civilian has had in recent years. Due to his association with the Admiralty he was returning to Canada on the *Rodney* when the *Bismarck* incident occurred. They doubled back and he was in on the kill of the *Bismarck*. His story is a most interesting one as he had a grand-stand seat through the whole show.

Dr Green and Mr Kuhring are marooned temporarily at the Azores but should be back in a few days when we will get more interesting information as to what we can do in the aeronautical field.

The Rockefeller Foundation have given us $7,500 to assist Canadian scientists who wish to visit the United States. This will be a useful thing as the universities are finding it difficult to send their scientists to meetings in the United States due to the restriction of foreign exchange.

As you know, because there are such a number of visiting scientists in England, there is a demand for the establishment of a scientific liaison office in England at Canada House. Our great difficulty is in finding the proper people to send. Nearly everyone has volunteered to go, but most of our people who would be acceptable are doing work of the most vital importance here, and while we fully appreciate the necessity of such an office we consider the most essential thing is for us to produce actual results here. However, we are canvassing the matter and will make a selection in a few days.

The chemical-warfare work is going along well and the actual work has started on the experimental field in Alberta. The organization has been set up and while the administrative director will be an officer of the Department of Defence, the actual administration of the real technical work will be done by Davies, Maass, Flood, etc. Maass has done remarkable work in the chemical field, has placed Canada in the first rank, and is one of the most energetic and productive people I have ever met. He wants to go to England again but I hesitate as he carries the most extraordinary load of detailed work, as well as general supervision of all the work across Canada, and his liaison with the United States is most valuable. He takes no holidays at all and works on an average of sixteen hours a day. I know of no one whose heart is more in the war or who is using his abilities and talents more effectively.

I was down to Kingston at the meeting of the Royal Society when we were both made Fellows at Large, and there was great enthusiasm when your citation and fellowship were announced.

I had a pleasant trip to Halifax where I combined business with pleasure and it was gratifying to see the appreciation of the fighting services for the work the council is doing.

The ceremony at McGill, where I got a D Sc was interesting; Dorothy Thompson was given an honourary degree and made an excellent speech. Honourary degrees were also given to Her Royal Highness, Princess Alice, His Excellency Hu Shih, the Chinese ambassador to Washington, and Rt Hon Malcolm MacDonald. While I got the degree, I felt that it was a recognition of the work of the council and that I was getting it in your place.

All the staff of the council wish to be remembered to you, and my wife joins me in sending best wishes and regards to Mrs McNaughton and yourself.

Sincerely yours

C.J. Mackenzie

HQ Canadian Corps
2 July 1941

Dear Dean Mackenzie:

This is just a line to acknowledge your letter of 19 June 1941, which
reached me today and which I have just read through with the great
interest that I always find in all communications from yourself.

Brigadier Kenneth Stuart has just arrived by air and he has also been
giving me a short account of the recent developments at home. Your ears
must have burned with the praise which he gives to the work of the
National Research Council and particularly of yourself and of Dr Maass.

As regards the organization of liaison with this country, I do think it
would be well to place some of the council's men in the London office of
the Canadian Ministry of Supply. Mr C.A. Banks, who is in charge of this
office, is most sympathetic to the proposal and I understand he has cabled
Mr Howe advice that it should be done in the very near future.

My wife joins me in sending kindest regards to yourself and Mrs
Mackenzie, and with best wishes to all.

Very sincerely yours

A.G.L. McNAUGHTON

Ottawa
2 August 1941

Dear General McNaughton:

I received your letter of July 2 and was glad to hear from you and to learn
that you find interest in the informal news-letters which I have been
sending you.

I have not seen Brigadier Kenneth Stuart since he got back but have
heard indirectly of his trip and hope to see him within a few days.

The matter of liaison has given me considerable thought. We have
finally decided to send Dr Howlett to London and have associated with
him Mr [A.H.R.] Smith who is already there, and they can pick up what
clerical staff is required. I discussed the matter with the minister and the
deputy minister of Munitions and Supply, as to whether our liaison office
should be attached to Canada House or Mr Banks's office. There seemed

to me to be certain advantages in having it attached to Mr Banks's organization, but on the other hand the High Commissioner in England and the
Department of External Affairs were strong in their opinion that it should
be attached to Canada House. As the liaison officers have to deal not only
with the Department of Munitions and Supply but with the Air Force, the
Admiralty, and the medical people, it was decided that for the present at
least our liaison should be attached to the High Commissioner's Office,
although that should not in any way affect the closest associations with Mr
Banks's office.

I had thought that it might have been possible for me to go to England
for a short time and I actually had passage booked on one of the bombers,
but the situation here is such that I am not happy about leaving the office
even for a matter of a few weeks. Problems seem to arise almost daily
which, if not attended to, would hold up our essential work, and since
coming here almost two years ago I have not felt free to take any holidays
and have never been away from the office over a few days at a time.

You will realize what the set-up here is and how unsuited are the
seconds in command, and while I do not wish to over-emphasize my own
activities it is almost certain that if I were away for any particular length of
time things which I normally attend to would not be done or, perhaps
worse, be done in a way which would not be in the best interests of the
council. For instance, last Tuesday at a meeting of the War Technical and
Scientific Development Committee, it was decided that the RDF development work which that committee had supported up until the present to
the extent of $350,000 had become so thoroughly proven that the gov-
ernment should provide the necessary financing in the future. As our
appropriation in the War Technical and Scientific Development Committee was almost spent, and as we have existing commitments of three
hundred thousand dollars against this project and a staff of 150 which
must be paid monthly, it was necessary for me to get prompt action. I
might say that yesterday morning I met the finance minister and succeeded in getting a further grant of seven hundred thousand dollars for
the balance of the fiscal year.

While our work is going along in a most satisfactory way, it is a constant
battle to overcome the difficulties inherent in a democracy. For instance,
three weeks ago in a perfectly commendable endeavour to prevent the
civil service from taking large numbers of young men of military age, an
Order in Council was passed saying that no government department
could hire any man of military age (which apparently extended from
nineteen to forty-five) excepting on a special permit from the Civil Service

Commission. This Order in Council, intended for one purpose, had the effect in an indirect way of placing the Research Council under the Civil Service Commission as to the appointment of employees. It took me two weeks to get a new Order in Council put through exempting the Research Council from the restrictions under the previous one.

I just point these things out to indicate the type of problem which is constantly arising, which can be solved if one is on the spot but which, if permitted to go for some long time, would seriously affect the efficiency and enthusiasm of the workers here.

The work of the Radio Committee has been, I think, amazingly successful. We have now produced a GL 3 equipment which is being used as a prototype for an order of four hundred through the lease-lend arrangement with the United States. I think our friends in England and the United States were skeptical and thought we could not do this but last week we had a most satisfactory demonstration in Ottawa. The United States Army officers brought twenty-six of the chief engineers and designing engineers from the Bell Laboratories, Westinghouse, General Electric and Sperry Corporation up to see the equipment which we had developed. We put on a demonstration and held an aeroplane accurately in the field for one and a half hours without losing it once, although it manoeuvred, changed elevation, distance, azimuth, etc., continually. The chief engineer of the American Westinghouse Company told Colonel Phillips in Toronto afterwards that his company, which has had more experience in this particular field than any other in the United States and which is actually working on similar development, would not have believed that what we had done in nine months could have been done in under two years, and the American group said that if their organizations had done as much and as satisfactory work as we had done in the last nine months they would consider the construction of a million-dollar building on our farm justified. Incidentally, we have two buildings on that site which cost fifty thousand dollars, and a number of tents and other shacks.

We have groups today both in Boston and in Halifax fitting up naval vessels with RDF equipment and the work is growing apace. I feel that [J.T.] Henderson is being unjustly treated by the existing government regulations which prevent any promotions whatsoever in the permanent staff. Henderson has provided the drive and enthusiasm which has built up a section which is far larger and more active than the entire Physics Division was at the start of the war, and probably during next year we will expend well over one million dollars in this section alone. He has a staff including 115 from the Research Council and others from the services which brings the total to over 160, and many of them get quite good salaries, but it is absolutely impossible to raise Henderson's above the $3,300 which he was getting at the outbreak of war. Several of his men are in the same position and I feel more strongly about the matter because there is not a complaint out of any of them. They have been working every night now for the past two months and everyone who knows anything about the field at all is full of admiration for what this group has done.

Dr Rose's work with the Navy is also developing rapidly. We have a group of twelve in Halifax and are now establishing laboratories in Sydney, St John's, Newfoundland, and Vancouver. We have a good arrangement with the Navy and keep in intimate contact with everything that is being done in the United States.

The work in chemistry and chemical warfare is going rapidly and the field station in Alberta is underway. Flood has gone out there and probably will be in charge of that project when Mr Davies of Porton returns to England.

The gauge laboratory is going so well now that I rarely have occasion to visit it at all. I set it up as a special unit divorced from the Metrology Section but using that section in a consultant capacity, and the system is working out well. [J.S.] Johnson, who used to be with Grant, is now in charge and is doing well. Up to the present at least we can say that gauge examination has not held up production in any way.

I have just been able to negotiate for the construction of a high-explosives testing laboratory which will be run as a co-operative effort by the Research Council, the Department of Mines and Resources, the Department of National Defence, and the Department of Munitions and Supply and the Inspection Board. The building, which will cost sixty to seventy thousand dollars, will be built on our Montreal Road property. The Department of Mines and Resources will put in all their experimental testing equipment and supply three of their personnel. We will purchase the other necessary equipment and provide the money for operating personnel.

Parkin's new structures laboratory at the Montreal site is completed and his work on plastic plywood construction is going well. We have made many integral parts for aeroplanes and at the present time are building a complete Fleet 60 in plastic plywood construction so that we can compare performance, cost, etc. with a similar plane, made from metal, in use in Canada.

The buildings on the Montreal Road are practically finished and it is a most attractive group. The grounds are being levelled off by the Federal

District Commission staff and as soon as the rubbish is cleared out I will have some pictures taken and sent to you.

The work in medicine and aviation medicine is coming along nicely and Collip has taken over most of the work that Sir Frederick did. He is most energetic and enthusiastic and is very keen on the work of the council.

Dr W.H. Cook has done what I think is a clever bit of work in temporary refrigeration. As you know, the refrigeration space on boats is at a premium and the need for bacon in England great. At a conference with the Bacon Board, Cook suggested the possibility of insulating a bacon cargo by blowing cold air around the cargo. The board was willing to take a gamble on a million pounds of bacon and Cook had ten days to develop the equipment and install it in the boat. He worked night and day, had special units made, arranged the cargo in the boat, conduits, etc., installed the equipment and had one of his men go with the boat to Father Point. We just have a report from England that the cargo got there in good condition and Dr Cook is now in Montreal arranging for another cargo involving two million pounds of bacon. The portable units which he rigged up only cost a fraction of a per cent of the value of the bacon, and if not recoverable, the loss is not great. The idea was relatively simple but entirely original and we feel very happy over the results.

I am glad to hear from our many mutual friends who have seen you recently that you appear to be in the best of health and spirits.

My wife joins me in sending kindest regards to Mrs McNaughton and yourself.

Yours sincerely

C.J. MACKENZIE

HQ Canadian Corps
29 July 1941

Dear Dean Mackenzie:

This is just a line to acknowledge your letter of 7 July 1941, which was given me a few days ago by Lieut-Col K.S. Maclachlan, acting deputy minister of National Defence (Naval Service). He also gave me a sample of the first melt of optical glass produced by Research Enterprises Limited.

This seems to be of most excellent quality and I trust that its production marks another substantial step forward in the matter of starting the production of gun sights, etc., in Canada.

Col Maclachlan showed me the Canadian Naval List which records the close relations which you have managed to establish with his department, and he was very emphatic on the great service being rendered by yourself and by the members of the National Research Council staff; in this connection he referred especially to Rose, Ballard, and [George] Field. You can well imagine the deep satisfaction I take, personally, in hearing of all this good work and I offer you my sincerest congratulations on the success which has attended your efforts.

As regards the radio fuse, I was interested in Shenstone's report dated 28 May 1941, which shows the lines you are working on and the prospects of success which have become evident.

I have not been able to keep closely in touch with this phase of the work in England, but periodically I visit HQ Air Defence of Great Britain to learn what is going on. The most promising project here seems to be the radio fuse tripped by impulse from the ground when the cathode-ray images of the target and of the shell are coincident on the screen. This is a most secret development and in several trials excellent results have been obtained. I think the method is intrinsically sounder than any of those based on proximity effects, whether optical, electrical, or acoustic.

Progress with the high-velocity conical gun is not as rapid as I would wish, but at last the Ordnance Board is moving, although very slowly. I do hope that you will take this project in hand and get us a solution.

With kindest regards to all at the National Research Council and with best wishes to yourself, in which my wife joins,

Very sincerely yours

A.G.L. McNAUGHTON

Ottawa
14 August 1941

Dear General McNaughton:

I received your letter of July 29 and have also seen Brigadier [Guy] Turner and Colonel Maclachlan, who brought word directly of you and the grand work which you are doing. We all, I think, feel more pleased that you think well of the work that the council has been able to do than of anything else, and it is impossible for me to speak too highly of the splendid co-operation which everyone has given us and of the tireless enthusiasm and devotion to duty of the entire staff.

There is no doubt in my mind that what success we are having is the result of long years of sound preparation and those of us who have had the opportunity of working with such an institution in this crisis are fortunate indeed.

Brigadier Turner said that you were particularly interested in obtaining reports on the high-velocity projectiles and on the preparation of high explosives in Canada, and I am writing this note to report on these two projects.

Mr Parkin has the high-velocity-projectile problem under way with the object of developing a projectile with a muzzle velocity of the order of 5,000 feet per second. It is planned to undertake the study in two stages, first, the development of a stable unrotated projectile, and, second, the increase of muzzle velocity by the use of tapered unrifled barrels and skirted projectiles.

In stage one, an unrifled Bofors 40 mm barrel has been secured and a simple breech-block firing mechanism and mount will be designed and fitted to the barrel. Experimental projectiles are being designed and will be made and fired. The projectiles will be made as light as possible and the propellant charge will be increased to the limit of safety in order to attain a high muzzle velocity. The projectiles will be directed through aligned, cross-sectioned, paper or fabric screens placed at suitable intervals up to 1,000 yards ranged to check the stability of flight, and velocities will be measured by a chronograph developed and made by Dr Rose.

Preliminary study is being given to stage number two but actual work has not started yet. The development work will be in charge of Mr Klein, assisted by Lieutenant Ian McKay, Baker (a draftsman), and an effort is being made to secure the release of J.L. McGregor of the RCAF, who seems well fitted along this line of work. Our greatest difficulty on this project at the present time is to obtain well-qualified men and there is a possibility that Lieutenant McKay will be recalled by the Navy. However, we are making every effort to obtain suitable staff and will not let up on our efforts on this project.

We will also keep you informed of the progress of the program in the hope that you will forward comments and criticism.

For your confidential information the United States authorities are embarking on a similar study and I have invited the director of that project to come to Ottawa next week. He is an enthusiastic and able experimentalist and has large funds at his disposal. He is anxious to have the closest co-operation with our group. When he arrives here we will have a conference of all parties who have any knowledge of the problem and I am sure that if you have any ideas for experimental work which are beyond our resources that we could probably encourage our American friends to undertake any promising program.

Dr Maass has given me a report on the recent developments of RDX [Research Department Explosives] in Canada and I think you will be interested in what has been done in this field. This is another case of where the council has been able to make a valuable contribution, I think to the surprise of our English friends who gave little encouragement to Dr Maass in the first instance. The work at McGill and Toronto is promising and is now entering the stage where pilot plants are being constructed at both Toronto and Montreal, and if thought advisable full-scale production should be a possibility in the near future.

Dr Howlett expected to leave for England before this but has been laid up with an old complaint for the past ten days. He, happily, is practically recovered now and probably will go next week. He is taking a complete list of our projects and will be able to give you much first-hand information. I hope his office in England will be successful.

We just heard a few hours ago that Prime Minister Churchill and President Roosevelt had been in conference for three days on the Atlantic, and it seems that much good will come out of this epoch-making meeting.

Everyone who returns from England brings most flattering reports of the work you are doing and we in Canada feel very proud on that account.

With kindest regards from all of us at the National Research Council.

Sincerely yours

C.J. MACKENZIE

Ottawa
15 September 1941

Dear General McNaughton:

I have just had a letter from Dr Howlett and he tells me how extraordinarily kind and generous you have been in seeing that he meets the proper people in England and gets off to a good start. When we were considering the establishment of an office, some of my advisers suggested that it would be well to send a very senior officer to England to be in charge of our office so that he could get entrée to the highest officials there. I drew attention to the fact that the president of the National Research Council was not only the Officer Commanding the Canadian forces in England but one of the most highly thought of scientists and soldiers in the United Kingdom, that if we sent a competent scientist from our own staff no one could go to England with better introductions than you could give, and I felt sure you would do what you have done. I am also in hope that our office will be of some benefit to you, and it is needless for me to assure you that I have told Howlett we will consider it a privilege to do anything possible. We are quite prepared to send any of our experts to England at any time you suggest it.

At the present time we are planning on sending Mr Ballard over for a brief trip as he is anxious to obtain the latest information in connection with the projects which he is working on for the Navy and the Army. Later on Sanders and another one of our staff will go over when we send our first GL 3 prototype.

You have probably heard something of the work of the Radio Section and the indications are that we have scored rather well in this field. We will spend about one million dollars in this section this year and in the estimates for next year I am asking for one million, two hundred thousand dollars for the Radio Section alone. As you know we have actually installed equipment on the Atlantic coast on warships, etc., but our greatest accomplishment, I think, is in the construction of a GL 3 set which, as you know, is the RDF end of an anti-aircraft assembly consisting of radio locator, predictor, and guns. We undertook the development of this set about a year ago and I think it is safe to say that few people in Britain thought we could do anything about it at all; in fact, many such as Sir Frank Smith pooh-poohed the idea of anything coming out of Canada. The United States were also working on similar equipment and when we intimated that we were about ready to go into production there was a great stir in all quarters. We actually got an order for about thirty million dollars' worth of equipment through the lend-lease arrangement and then the United Kingdom authorities seemed to come to life. We have had one set inspected by nearly everyone on the American continent, and the American scientists and chief engineers from Westinghouse, General Electric, Sperry, Bell Laboratories, etc., have all been up for demonstrations and have expressed amazement that we have been able to do in ten months what none of the other countries has achieved.

The British authorities have been skeptical from time to time about the performance of our set, and in fact we have had little else but veiled criticism from them. Only last week Professor [N.L.] Oliphant, who was in the United States, suggested that it was absolutely silly to think that a set could be made in Canada. However, he came to Canada, we put on a demonstration for him, and he and Sir Lawrence Bragg actually conducted a test of the accuracy of the tracking of the set. When they were through, Oliphant said the accuracy of our set was much better than anything in England and that with a slight modification we could make it almost perfect. We have had one set operating constantly for a month now, another set is being delivered to Research Enterprises Limited by parts, and we have three more sets under way, one of which will be sent to England as soon as it is ready. We had hoped to get this set off before now but we are being held up by the lack of delivery of certain mechanical gear which is being made outside of the Research Council, and this delay is part of the general difficulties of industrial production. When we are ready to send the set over, Sanders and at least one other man will go with it and the indications are that it will be subjected to critical examination. ...

There is another matter which is under consideration but on which no decision has been reached, that is, the method of handling RDF inquiries and liaison in England. As you know the RDF work touches all of the services and in Canada the Chiefs of Staff committee have placed in a subcommittee the control and handling of all RDF matters, from scientific development through production to tactical use. The committee consists of two members from each of the services, Research Enterprises, and the National Research Council, and I am the chairman. The committee is functioning quite smoothly; we have been able to iron out most of the difficulties and I think it is fair to say that everyone is co-operating most heartily. In the committee the other day the members of the services made the suggestion that it might be wise to have our liaison work in England done under the auspices of the committee here, that is, to have a group in England consisting of representatives of the Research Council and an officer from each of the services who would work together in the obtaining and passing on of information. The service officers pointed out that when in England and assigned to this work they also have other duties at Military Headquarters which make it impossible for them to co-operate as effectively as desirable. As a result of the discussion the proposal is being placed before the Chiefs of Staff committee with the request that they give the proposal serious consideration.

Work on the high-velocity projectile is progressing as rapidly as possible. Parkin is having difficulty obtaining staff these days but he is well into the first stage of his investigation and has plans drawn and production arranged for the first aerodynamically controlled projectile. The unrifled Bofors gun has been delivered and the mounting is being constructed. For your confidential information, I had a long session with Dr [Roger] Adams of the Carnegie Geophysics Laboratory in Washington who had been assigned this general project by the NDRC of the United States, and he is laying plans for a most comprehensive study. He is starting on the basis that the erosion problem is a fundamental one and that if a more conventional design of guns is ultimately to be useful, it will be necessary to solve the erosion problem first. Without much expert knowledge myself, it seems to me that Dr Adams's investigation is a long-term one and, while it is undoubtedly worth while doing, the approach which you have in mind has greater chances of more immediate success.

Sir Lawrence Bragg will be returning to England next week and we will all be sorry to have him go, as he has been most helpful and he has become very popular with everyone on this side. We do not know who his successor will be. A suggestion has been made that Geoffrey Hill of Pye's directorate would be a suitable man and we would welcome this proposal, as we have had no one to date who is a specialist in aeronautical engineering, but unfortunately Hill is temporarily laid up with duodenal ulcers and will not be available for a few months. Professor George Thomson of the Imperial College of London is at present in the United States, and is actually in Ottawa today, and there has been the suggestion that he might serve as a liaison officer for a period. Sir Lawrence has intimated that he will try to get an appointment with you when he goes back, and he can give you a clear picture of many of our detailed projects.

I am in the middle of an extremely busy time as there are several important committee meetings this week. The Review Committee meets on Tuesday, we have a council meeting on Wednesday, Dr Matthews of the Air Ministry arrives on Thursday and on Friday we have an all-day meeting of the Committee on Aviation Medicine, as well as a visit from Lister of the BAC [British Air Commission] in Washington. On Saturday I am planning to take a hurried trip to the west. As you know I have not been away from Ottawa for more than a few days since I came here, but I feel that I must visit the west now as the chemical-warfare field north of Medicine Hat is in operation and I want to see it. Also, we have work in all of the western universities and a station in Vancouver working with the Admiralty, and I have never seen any of these projects. It will be a strenuous trip as I am also president of the Engineering Institute of

Canada this year and will probably have to speak at a number of meetings on the way. The chemical-warfare section at Medicine Hat fortunately has four aeroplanes and the superintendent has indicated that one of them will be available to me in the west, which will help somewhat.

We were very interested and excited about the raid on Spitsbergen; I was particularly interested as my old friend Brigadier Potts was the commanding officer. I presume that all the boys were a bit disappointed that there was not a bit of a scrap, but that will not doubt come in good time.

My wife joins me in sending kindest regards to Mrs McNaughton and yourself.

Yours sincerely

C.J. MACKENZIE

HQ Canadian Corps
11 October 1941

Dear Dean Mackenzie:

I am afraid I have been remiss in replying to your letters of August 2, August 14, and September 15. This is the first time for many weeks that I have had an opportunity to sit down to dictate a letter other than those concerned with the day-by-day routine of the corps.

As regards the liaison office, Dr Howlett is now settled down in an office on St James Square with Smith as his assistant and they are covering an immense range of useful work. I have not had much time to give to him but I have tried, whenever possible, to bring him into contact with the people at the head of research in the various departments and I feel that he has taken every advantage of this to develop matters for himself. I hear nothing but praise for his efforts on all sides. In consequence, I think that you can feel that this venture is now well launched and that the council will get most useful results from it.

Am very glad to hear that Parkin is proceeding with the high-velocity gun. I have now been able to induce the Board of Ordnance here to authorize the construction of a gun somewhat on the same lines, so that shortly we should be experimenting with these matters in both places. I do hope that Parkin will keep Dr Howlett informed so that he can pass the results on to the Board of Ordnance direct.

As regards research on methods of producing RDX, the visit of [Dr J.H.] Ross and [Dr H.S.] Sutherland was, I think, useful. I had a short talk with them myself when I outlined the need of finding some compound with very much greater power. I afterwards had a talk with Sir Robert Robinson. He made one suggestion that I passed on to Dr Howlett to send on to Dr Maass and yourself.

The particular problem in respect to co-ordination of research information for Canada which we have is in relation to the information about RDF and GL equipments. Over here the Army, Navy, Air Force, Munitions and Supply, and Dr Howlett are concerned and, as far as I can determine, no one individual, representative of these services, can secure a comprehensive picture. Also, there is much overlapping in demands on British departments for information, which they resent. I have suggested to Dr Howlett that we should arrange for Mr Massey to call a meeting of representatives of all concerned to try to work out a system of co-ordination, and I think that this will be arranged shortly.

As regards the Canadian GL Mk 3 which Dr Sanders is to bring over, I went over your letter of 15 September with Dr Howlett and asked him to cable you offering to provide the technical staff and operators to help Dr Sanders in demonstrating this equipment. We have about 190 officers and other ranks trained in various technical capacities relating to this gear and I have no doubt we will be able to pick out enough to meet all requirements. You may be sure that we are anxious to assist in every way possible.

Things go on here much as usual and the morale of the troops is being well maintained despite the difficulties inherent in remaining alert and on guard over long periods.

My wife joins me in kindest regards to yourself and Mrs Mackenzie and to the members of the council and staff.

Very sincerely yours

A.G.L. McNaughton

Ottawa
27 October 1941

Dear General McNaughton:

I received your letter of October 11 and was delighted to get it. I am always amazed that you can find time to write about matters back here when you are so busy in England.

We are all pleased with the way our liaison office is working in London and Dr Howlett was indeed most fortunate that you were able to launch him in the effective way you did. He has been sending a steady flow of reports, material, questions, etc., and is doing a very effective job as far as we are concerned and, I think, from the reports I hear, from the standpoint of the corresponding stations in England.

I made a hurried trip through the west last month for the purpose of visiting the various universities and scientific stations, and while it was rather hectic I feel that the results were well worth while. We now have research projects in every university in Canada and are trying to do more in that line all the time but it is, as you know, difficult to farm out problems in our major fields of activity.

The chemical-warfare section is going well. The experimental station at Suffield, Alberta, has been delayed owing to non-completion of contracts for equipment of laboratories. As you probably know we are beginning to feel the industrial pinch in Canada now and are having great difficulties with deliveries, priorities, etc. Everyone, even the government, I think, is doing now what I recall you recommended in 1939, that is, conducting plans and thinking on the basis of man-hours, power, equipment, and supplies available rather than on dollars and cents. We in the council are now in the position where we have to turn down work and make careful selections of projects for the simple reason that we have not available the man-hours to do everything that comes to us. This is particularly true in the shops where we have to compete with industry for men, and where our government regulations make it almost impossible for us to compete in salaries. While I am perfectly aware of the inherent difficulties in government administration, the unintentional delays and obstructions that occur are almost heart-breaking at times. Poor Parkin is having an awful time with his prevailing-rates people, who should be on the same wage basis as ordinary industry, particularly the ones who are on war work, but the government's labour policy, both internally and externally, is far from being clarified. There is, as you know, a ban on promotions, and we have great difficulties in this regard as the men of the same qualification and doing the same civilian type of work, either in the forces in Canada or in industry, are paid usually much higher rates than we can pay. We are always being faced with the loss of men. As a matter of fact we have had eighty-two separations in the last sixty days. Incidentally, I am enclosing a statement showing the number of employees working either directly for the council or on associate committees, etc., and their distribution. When one realizes that the total numbers for 1939 were about three hundred and that now we are over one thousand, it is easy to appreciate that there would be growing pains.

Another of our difficulties is in connection with our liaison officers in England. I tried to get protection for Howlett, Smith, and any of the other boys who go over on a basis comparable to the protection afforded the armed forces. I had an Order in Council prepared which would give to people like Howlett, Ballard, and Rose, in case of death, protection to their families equivalent to what a major in the infantry receives. I thought the Order in Council was through but found that it was held up; subsequently an Order in Council was passed which gives to all civilians who are killed or injured by enemy action in England the protection and pension rates equivalent to a lieutenant in the Army. This, to my mind, is grossly unfair and presents a real problem. A.H.R. Smith has a wife and three small children and, as he is a war appointee of the council, he has no pension benefits from the government. In case of death his wife would be left with $840 a year to support herself and bring up and educate three children. The result is that, with the best wishes in the world, she feels that he should be recalled. As you know, we are constantly sending our people to England and as men like Ballard, Rose, Green, etc., are all young married men without any financial resources, I may try to see if I can get some protection through the Department of Defence for them while they are in England.

The Canadian GL Mark III which we are sending to you will be ready shortly. We would have been able to ship it the end of this month but for the unexpected delay in some of the equipment which was being supplied by other manufacturers. However, we are hoping to get it away early in November. We are proud of the set and of the achievement of the council in this respect. As you know, we at the council are making five sets: no. 1, which after further experimental work will be turned over to the Army in Canada; no. 2, a prototype for Research Enterprises Limited; no. 3, to be sent to Britain for demonstration; no. 4 for the Canadian Army, and no. 5 to be sold to the United States Army. The scientific officers in the various stations in England have been most anxious to get our set sent over at the earliest moment. As they only wanted it uder loan, and as the commercial cost is about $60,000 and the cost to us about $100,000 or $120,000, we decided that the best way would be to send it to you, and the financial accounting then could be done in Canada between ourselves and the Department of Defence here. Then you could permit it to be tested and examined by the various people in England who are particularly interested. I do hope that the set gets over in good condition and that the tests are satisfactory. We are trying to make arrangements to have it sent on a battleship, and Dr Sanders and one of the technical staff will probably fly.

Brigadier Guy Turner was in to see me the other day and I took him out to the aeronautical laboratories to show him your high-velocity project. You will be interested to know that the three hand-made projectiles are now ready and we are arranging to have them fired in Petawawa next week. Horton is arranging equipment to photograph the trials so that we can have a record of the performance of the projectiles.

For your confidential ears, you will be interested to know that there is now a definite feeling in many of the scientific departments of government, who are outside the orbit of the Research Council, that they would like to be within our organization. I feel that after the war there will probably be some comprehensive reorganization of all departmental scientific activities here. I was approached the other day by [V.W.T.] Scully, commissioner of Customs, who wants us to take over the Customs Laboratory. He told me that he and his officers realize that it would be a much better arrangement if we would look after the scientific direction of their laboratories, as he was well aware of the fact that not only on the basis of cost but from the standpoint of maintaining high standards of technique and well-qualified personnel, a small detached laboratory could not compete with an institution such as ours. Fortunately, the head of his laboratory is retiring this year and he thinks there will be no difficulty in making the transfer. Dr Steacie is having a meeting with Commissioner Scully and some of his officers tomorrow and I think probably we will take the laboratory over shortly. We will have to leave the laboratory where it is at the present time as nearly every square foot of available space in our building is now being used, but after the war it may be possible to rearrange the analytical laboratories and find space for it here. Scully has a budget of about one hundred thousand dollars for his laboratory; his proposal is that they merely hand over the appropriation to us and that we will take over all of their equipment, accommodation, and all of the members of the staff that we can take without embarrassment. He agrees that if there are one or two odd cases that would obstruct the essential reorganization, he will find positions for such people elsewhere. I think you will agree with me that it is important that we should undertake this work. I think it is definitely in the interests of scientific work and the government that all of the work should be done on the high plane that will be guaranteed by National Research Council supervision.

The work in medicine is going along well. The co-operation is splendid and Collip is doing conscientious and effective work as Banting's successor. [W.G.] Penfield has just returned from a two months' trip to England and is enthusiastic about the work that is being done. The meetings of both of the associate medical committees are always interesting and vital. I believe the work which you started in medical research to be one of the important scientific contributions made by the council for some time.

I was down to the Queen's Centenary last week and we all got a great thrill out of your recorded speech, which came over just as clear and natural as if you had been standing on the platform. The whole occasion was a very pleasant one, and there were over three hundred delegates from outside institutions there.

My wife joins me in sending very best wishes and kindest regards to you and Mrs McNaughton.

Yours sincerely

C.J. MACKENZIE

Ottawa
6 December 1941

Dear General McNaughton:

In common with all Canadians from coast to coast, we at the Research Council were much disturbed at the first reports that you were suffering from an illness which made it necessary for you to take a rest. We have been relieved by information from headquarters that your illness was not serious and that you will be back on duty soon. I do hope that you are feeling fit again by this time.

Affairs at the council are going on reasonably well. Nearly every day brings some new problems and we continue to enlarge. We have at the present time about one thousand employees, including those in the various research stations across Canada, as well as our own staff here. The complexion of our work changes from time to time and only two days ago I was able to get an interview with the Treasury Board in an attempt to iron out some difficulties in connection with our shops. I pointed out to them that before the war we had a total of about forty mechanics on the staff of the council, fifteen of whom were on an annual salary basis and the remainder on an hourly prevailing-wage basis, but that now we had one hundred and forty mechanics and were operating the equivalent of an industrial shop working on problems for the Departments of Defence, Munitions and Supply, etc., and that we could not operate under the restrictions of the normal peace-time civil service regulations. I found the board particularly sympathetic and they granted every request I made.

Mr Ilsley has grown in stature with the war and I think is now one of the strong men in the Cabinet. The first Treasury Board meeting I went to he was acting Finance minister and obviously was considered one of the junior members of the Cabinet. The other day there was no question about the situation. He was the dominant and forceful character and, as far as I can see, the Treasury Board is Mr Ilsley. He granted me the right to pay straight overtime to our salaried mechanics, to pay time and a half to our prevailing-rate mechanics, and to adjust the salaries of the prevailing-rate mechanics automatically as the Department of Labour adjusts the prevailing rates for this district. There was some hesitation in granting the time and a half because of conflict with the policy in vogue in other departments, but Mr. Ilsley said, 'I am disposed to grant the request of the Research Council because I think it is fair and reasonable and they have not been in the habit of asking for things which were not necessary.'

I might say that the entire wage policy has been serious and a source of great trouble to everyone. No doubt the Department of Labour has great difficulties but there are many who think that they have not a sound grasp of the entire situation and are not sufficiently strong in their action. Many of our people are working long hours of overtime and the radio section has been working sixty-five hours a week for three or four weeks now in order to get the GL set off to England, which probably will arrive about the time this letter does. The same strenuous time has been experienced in most departments and we often see the wear and tear of such conditions on the nerves, but on the whole things are going smoothly.

The industrial and economic picture is tightening all the time and the obtaining of priorities on equipment and supplies is now a major problem, as it is almost impossible to get material excepting for urgent war work. Our priority difficulties are largely in connection with the United States, and I had a fight on my hands to get a rating for the Research Council. In the United States their Research Council and universities have a low priority rating and the United States authorities carried that low rating over to us, owing to our name. However, after some work and with the help of a number of friends, we were able to establish in the minds of the Priorities Board in Washington the character of the work we were doing, and we now have an A1A rating which is eminently satisfactory. Even with this rating we have to make application for every specific item, and effective priorities will only be given on that part of our work which is judged of extreme importance for war purposes.

During the last couple of months I have visited a number of the industrial centres where war work is going on and the picture is quite interesting. One gets the impression that in a plant such as the Ford Motor Company, where vehicles and Bren-gun carriers are being turned out, the organization is most effective and impressive, probably because they are working along familiar lines. In some of the other plants, however, where additions have been made for war purposes, one gets the feeling that the operations are not as efficient as they might be, and in some cases one suspects that the civilian peace-time activities of the concern get more expert and serious attention than the war activities. However, I think this phase is passing and on the whole there is a remarkable lot of first-class work under way.

I was particularly struck with the work at the Quebec Arsenal, where they have a large program and seem to be doing a splendid job.

Before this letter reaches you, you no doubt will have seen Rose and Ballard. The latter we know has reached England and Rose is somewhere on his way. From them you can get an accurate picture of our work in physics.

The work in chemistry is going along well indeed and Maass has done a most extraordinary job. He is one of the most efficient and effective men I have met. He says very little, works long hours, wastes no time on trivial details, and gets things done. He is popular with everyone he meets and it is interesting to see how the chemistry departments of Toronto and McGill are working together under Maass's general guidance. There is not the slightest bit of jealousy and they all work as one team. To go with Maass to Toronto, you would think he was one of their staff, and the same is true when [George] Wright or Gordon go to McGill.

The most recent development in chemical warfare is the resignation of Colonel Morrison, director of Chemical Warfare, and his replacement by Maass. Maass was reluctant to take on the job but I urged him to do so, as he is responsible for the general technical direction at any rate and if the wrong man were put in by the Department of National Defence our excellent relationships might deteriorate. We feel that it would be better for Maass to retain his connection with the council and run the directorate from the Research Council building and he proposes to do this. He will, of course, have officers of the Department of National Defence under him who can look after the strictly military aspects of the organization.

In the Physics Division the activity continues. The gauge laboratory is running so smoothly that I hardly know it exists. After some preliminary difficulties because it was trying to operate as a section of the Division of Physics, I set up what amounts to an independent organization with J.S. Johnson in charge. Johnson, you may remember, was a junior electrical engineer. He is proving to be an excellent administrator and the fact that there has been no suggestion anywhere of a hold-up in this end of the game is in itself, I think, significant.

The Radio Section is, of course, a great problem as it will next year spend about fifty per cent more than the entire Research Council did before the war. Including one hundred service people, we have a staff of about two hundred and fifty and it is a large-scale operation. I have had many headaches in this section, as you can see the absurdity of having an organization like that trying to function as a section of one division of the council. Personalities have entered the picture, which you can imagine would, and it has been difficult to get the section running with the enterprise and energy which is necessary and at the same time on a reasonably sound basis. Some time ago I divorced the business relationships from the director's office in the interests of efficiency and we are now trying to work out some organization which will permit this unit to operate more as a unit detached from the ordinary routine of the division. If one only knew what the future developments were to be, it would be easy to build up an organization in the first instance that would be satisfactory.

The optics laboratory is busy and Horton is doing extraordinarily well.

George Field is fitting into the picture well and is easy to work with. Rose, of course, is doing excellent work with the Navy and electrical engineering is likewise being effective. Niven is doing some work on heat and R.H. Field valuable work on design and metrology. Altogether, the section heads of this division are competent and able young men and they are all doing excellent work.

Cook in biology has done some first-rate work and his developments in temporary refrigeration are ... something that we are all proud of.

Parkin's division is going along nicely but we are handicapped in that field by the fact that the RCAF in Canada is essentially a training organization and their interest in research and operations, particularly in the higher brackets, is not a major one. However, we are now doing some useful work in connection with a training plane, the development of training devices, and the study of weaknesses appearing in machines in the training schools.

Kuhring is doing a lot of good work and is now working on the cooling system of the new scout car. The problems in gasolines, oils, and lubricants continue and we are making progress in the plastic-plywood aircraft construction.

Klein is pushing on with your HV work and has already had preliminary trials at Petawawa. He feels that it would be possible to stabilize an unrotated projectile. We are keeping all the pressure we can on him and his group, and Parkin is paying particular attention to it.

There is one very interesting but very secret development which only one or two of us know about. We have organized under the Research Council a section on cryptography which has succeeded in breaking down codes and cyphers and doing a really good job. It seems an unusual activity for the Research Council but the intelligence officers of the three services, the Mounted Police and the officers of External Affairs asked me if we could organize such a unit, as they thought we could probably do it easier and keep it under cover better than in any other way. I accordingly got a vote from the War Technical and Scientific Development Committee and we set up this unit. We have an associate committee consisting of the intelligence officers of the three services, the RCMP, a member from External Affairs and myself. We have an expert cryptographer from England and I look after the business arrangements, finances, etc. The secret-service material flows through the appropriate intelligence officers at the various headquarters.

We got into it in the first instance because our facilities were such that we could start a unit in a modest way to see whether or not it was a practicable thing to do. My feeling was that after we had done the organizing and got the staff trained, an official unit could be set up by the government to operate under one of the services or External Affairs. After six months of trial, when a decision had to be made as to how it should continue, all of the members were most insistent that they would prefer it to be carried on under our auspices and that will be done, for a while at least. It is pretty far from research but it is a most important and useful service.

We have at the Council a steady stream of visitors and His Excellency the Governor General is fond of coming to see us. I was to Government House at dinner on Wednesday night and he indicated that he would like to visit us again next week. I will take him out to the aeronautical laboratories on the Montreal Road this time.

One finds many friends who are willing to help as time goes on, and I have found Watson Sellar one of the best friends we have. As auditor general he is not tied up in the same way that other officials are and he is always willing and anxious to put his experience and advice at our disposal.

Mr MacKinnon, our minister, is also kindly disposed to us and, while he does not go into details, always he takes our advice and will sponsor any document we put up, fighting for us at council. Even Ronson seems kindly disposed and has actually given us considerable assistance recently in advice and suggestions as to how we could facilitate matters.

As this letter may not reach you much before Christmas, may I take this opportunity of conveying to you and Mrs McNaughton the very best wishes and compliments of the season from my wife and myself.
With kindest regards.

Yours sincerely

C.J. MACKENZIE

PS – Since dictating the above, three interesting things have happened:

1. The GL set for England has been shipped from Ottawa and should be on the sea soon.

2. The CESA [Canadian Engineering Standards Association] at its annual meeting today agreed to take over our 'fire hazards' approval work, thus bringing to fruition one of your carefully worked-out plans.

3. Canada in twenty-four hours has declared war on four nations: Romania, Hungary, Finland, Japan. The Japan treachery has united the United States for the first time behind belligerent action.   CJM

CMHQ
London
3 January 1942

Dear Dean Mackenzie:

Your most interesting letter of 6 December 1941 has just reached me and, needless to say, I have read it through with continuing and ever-growing satisfaction with the contribution that the council is making to Canada and the Empire and also to the United States in the troublous days through which we are passing at present.

May I say, too, how deeply and sincerely I congratulate you on what you have accomplished, for I do feel that the magnificent record largely finds its source and inspiration in yourself.

I will not attempt to comment on all the various points, but there are two or three matters I would like to mention. The first is in relation to Maass and the organization for chemical warfare which he now heads under the Defence Department. This is a satisfactory development and it will help us to clarify the situation at this end, which had become somewhat confused due to our uncertainty as to where Maass, Morrison, and others stood in the picture.

Some days ago I arranged for Howlett to meet the various people at CMHQ and the corps who are concerned in chemical-warfare matters, to discuss what we should do to bring order into the flow of information from the several sources here to you at the National Research Council, to the Defence Department, and to Suffield. It has been agreed that we will place a suitably qualified officer in the SD [Staff Duties] Branch at CMHQ to undertake the collection and forwarding of reports for the Defence Department, that the Ministry of Supply will continue to forward copies of all documents direct to Suffield, and that Howlett will be kept in the closest liaison with CMHQ.

Further, we will name an officer with appropriate experience to replace Rabinowitch on the Chemical Warfare Board and will name a doctor to keep close touch with the medical aspects of this work and to represent us on any related committees set up by the Medical Research Committee. Our mobile chemical-defence laboratory will now come directly under the GSO [General Staff Officer] 2 (CW) at Corps HQ for operations. All of this represents, I think, a solution for our past difficulties.

As regards the GL, this has now arrived safely and is being set up under Dr Sanders's arrangements and with all the assistance he requires from CMHQ and ADGB [Air Defence of Great Britain].

After some initial confusion with the Ministry of Supply, I think now that the views and wishes of all concerned have been harmonized and that all the difficulties and misunderstandings are out of the way. In this connection it was a great help to us to know that Colonel Wallace is officially associated with the Research Council and that he has your full confidence.

Sanders came over to England on the same ship with Crerar and they both, and Howlett as well, had dinner with my wife and me on Christmas Day. I was glad to see him and to hear at first hand something of the great work which has been going on in the council's radio laboratories under [J.T.] Henderson.

I have not seen Rose as yet but I am looking forward to a talk when he is somewhat less busy with his visits.

I am very happy that Klein's work with the high-velocity projectile shows possibilities of obtaining a stable form. The Ordnance Board project for the construction of a model of my sketch designs, copies of which have been sent on, has now been given a high priority and I have hopes that shortly their firing trials will commence.

I can well understand the friendship of Mr Ilsley, Mr MacKinnon and Watson Sellar for the council. These I would take for granted, but to bring Ronson around is a high triumph.

My wife joins me in kindest regards to yourself and Mrs Mackenzie and with our best wishes to all at the council.

Very sincerely yours

A.G.L. McNaughton

Ottawa
18 May 1942

My dear General McNaughton:

Ballard has just returned by Clipper and brings a very kind message from you and Mrs McNaughton. I am delighted to hear that you are in good health. I do hope that you will not overdo it again. We all feel that you are one of the all-too-few whose services we cannot afford to be without in a time of emergency.

Everything has gone on pretty much the same since you left Canada.* The Army Technical Development Board [ATDB] has had three meetings and Dick Harkness of the Northern Electric has taken over the directorship, at least for the present. There is quite a list of projects under way and no doubt the MGO has sent you the formal reports. I have been flirting with the idea of having Howlett attached to the Development Board as the

*McNaughton was in Canada during February 1942.

principal scientific officer when he returns, but of course that decision will have to be left until he gets to this country. I have a project before the board for the construction of a pilot plant for high explosives and propellants and have asked for a grant of three hundred thousand dollars to build the pilot plant, preferably in the vicinity of our explosives testing laboratory on the Montreal Road, and we hope to get under way within the next few weeks.

I made a visit to western Canada to inspect the chemical-warfare station at Suffield and it is a really good show. They have six laboratory buildings and housing accommodation for two hundred men. There is a good aerodrome and runway and about one-half dozen aeroplanes. There are artillery units, engineering units, and infantry units. You, of course, have had the official report of the large experiment which you requested and which was carried out in an impressive way. We stayed there three days and observed demonstrations and inspected the laboratories. I arranged to have two professors of chemistry there from each of the western universities and we have made arrangements for them to become associated with the scientific work, carry on various extramural projects, and act as consultants to the station. As there are also many problems in physics, engineering and meteorology, I have now made arrangements for the professors of physics at the three western universities to visit the station and make a similar contact.

Parkin's division is getting busy on wooden-aircraft schemes which are becoming active in Canada, and the glider situation is being gone into thoroughly. Klein is working hard on the high-velocity gun and Klein and Parkin are to confer with the mission from England which you mentioned in your most secret cable of a few days ago.*

We were all pleased to hear of the success of our GL equipment in England and appreciate your kindness and thoughtfulness in forwarding to us General Pile's message, which was very cheering. The Radio Section is going well and we are working more and more closely with the services every day.

Dr W.H. Cook has several investigations under way in connection with the manufacture of artificial rubber and is hopeful that one of his fermentation processes for making alcohol from wheat, as a stepping stone, at first, to butadiene and then to artificial rubber, will be successful.

*The mission, led by Geoffrey Pike, concerned the project known as 'Habakkuk.' Pike proposed to extend the limited range of land-based aircraft by constructing floating airports of ice; the scheme eventually proved to be as expensive as producing regular steel aircraft carriers, and was abandoned. See Eggleston, *Scientists at War*, pp. 153–59.

There has been a great deal of turmoil and recrimination in connection with the plebiscite vote* but I do hope affairs will settle down so that we in Canada may get on with our work.

There is one matter upon which I would like your advice. As you know, your seven-year appointment as president of the Research Council expires on June 1, 1942, and I am not sure whether you want the matter drawn to the attention of the government or not. You will recall that the Order in Council reads as follows: 'The undersigned therefore recommends that the said Major-General Andrew George Latta McNaughton, be appointed President of the National Research Council, for a period of seven years, dating from the first day of June, 1935, and until such time as his successor has been appointed.' The government would, of course, make no other appointments while you are overseas and by the terms of the contract your appointment would be automatically continued, but you may feel that it would be desirable to have an official renewal for another period of seven years. I thought it my duty to call this matter to your attention so that any action you may decide upon can be taken in the way that you would wish. I had thought at first that it might be proper for me to draw the attention of the minister to the situation, but on second thought I feel that it is more proper that I should call it to your attention for any action you deem wise.

The memories of the Engineering Institute banquet are fresh in the minds of all of us, and everyone is still talking of the great honour you did us and what an outstanding event it was.†

My wife joins me in sending kindest regards to Mrs McNaughton and yourself. With the best of wishes and hope for the future.

Yours sincerely

C.J. MACKENZIE

PS – I have just heard that you have been elected to honorary membership in the Institute of Electrical Engineers of Great Britain. May I offer my congratulations.   CJM

---

*On the question of conscription, interpreted for the voters by Mackenzie King in his famous phrase, 'Conscription if necessary, but not necessarily conscription.' The plebiscite had just been held, on 27 April 1942, and the vote was seventy per cent in favour. For McNaughton's involvement in the conscription issue, see Swettenham, vol. 2, pp. 191–192.

†During his visit to Canada in February 1942, McNaughton was the main speaker at this banquet.

Enc – Proceedings of the 138th Meeting of the Council, Ottawa, 19 March 1942.

Ottawa
14 July 1942

Dear General McNaughton:

First let me say how we all feel for you and Mrs McNaughton during this period when Ian is missing. We are all hoping and praying that good news will come any day now but in the meantime we do want you to know that you have our genuine and sincere sympathy.

The work at the council is proceeding reasonably well and we are increasing our staff almost daily until now we have over eleven hundred in and around this building and probably two or three hundred more at outside points.

In Parkin's division, Klein has been busy as a result of your cable on that most secret project.* He and Parkin were down for a conference with the Americans and British in Detroit last week and you will be interested to know that the report and knowledge which they were able to present on our experiences and experimental work on skis, etc., in Canada was much appreciated. You will also be interested to know that the Americans are pushing the project with great vigour, and prototypes of equipment have already been produced for test. In the aeronautical laboratories, Dr Green has now twenty-five projects under way and has been doing a great deal of valuable work in co-operation with the RCAF. There is a great deal of activity in connection with gliders and our structural laboratory, which has been working on plastic plywoods for a long time, has been of great value. We have taken on about fifteen more aeronautical engineers in Parkin's division and the volume of work turned out will increase rapidly. The de-icing crew is leaving for the west this week where they will carry out tests to investigate the various equipments developed to protect the engines, propellers, wind shields, wings, etc., from icing.

Howlett has been active since he got back in connection with aerial photography and as a result of a conference held at the National Research Council, Air Vice-Marshal Stedman has recommended to the Air Council that a photographic reconnaissance unit be formed in Canada and we are

*The secret project was the Weasel, a snowmobile eventually used for a wide variety of operations, including amphibious landings and negotiating mine fields.

all hoping that this will be done. In the meantime, actual experimental work on photographic problems is being continued.

You have probably seen Major-General [A.E.] Macrae and Brigadier G.P. Morrison, and no doubt have heard of what is happening in the Army Technical and Development Board. As you also have heard, Victor Sifton resigned as MGO and Assistant MGO Young has now been promoted to major-general and MGO. The organization under the board is gradually taking shape but, owing to the changes and the difficulty of obtaining a full-time director, has not moved as rapidly as we would all wish. There is also the difficulty that parts of the MGO's old functions are now in the Department of Munitions and Supply and, what is worse, are under two different directorates. I think that General Macrae feels that he should be head of all army design work in Munitions and Supply, while [R.E.] Jamieson really holds the position of director general of Army Engineering Design under Munitions and Supply, although he does not deal with guns and ammunition. Also, the relationship of Macrae to the Inspection Board is not as clear as it might be. As you know, the Inspection Board has a number of knowledgeable and competent people in Canada like Skentelbery and Ramsford. They also are building up an excellent scientific staff at the proving grounds at Valcartier and, within the last month, we have given them two excellent members of our staff for work on internal and external ballistics.

Rose at the National Research Council is the fire-control expert in Canada, from the theoretical standpoint at least, and as you know he and his staff have done a great deal of work on ballistics. In the gun-design section, Macrae has a large staff at Munitions and Supply and Klein has a staff of four or five at the NRC. Up to the present time there has been little co-ordination between these groups. In addition, on armour and projectiles, the Department of Mines and Resources, the National Research Council, the Inspection Board, and Munitions and Supply are all interested.

From all the above you will see that the real difficulty is getting this group operating as a unit, but there are really no insuperable difficulties and effective organization is, I think, only awaiting the return of Macrae and Morrison.

Our experts on ballistics and ammunition are now visiting Valcartier regularly and are advised of all the important shoots there, and the members of the scientific staff of the Inspection Board visit the Research Council every two weeks and go over our information. We are going to try to get the same co-operation in Klein's work on gun design and General Macrae's section. Rose, of course, works in close association with Morrison on fire-control work, and efforts are being made to get the four different interested parties in armour and projectile grouped in an effective way. I had a discussion with Mr Howe the other day and he said that his department would put up the money and support vigorously any worthwhile gun developments, so that, barring a decision as to what the General Staff requirements are, there should be no difficulty in getting on with the job.

The work in the Navy is expanding rapidly and new projects are arising every day. We are getting more intimate contact with the British Navy and I think the fact that we are having their key men come to see us more frequently suggests that they have an increasing confidence in us and an appreciation of what we can do. Within the last few weeks we have had Mr Wright, DSR [Director, Scientific Research], Admiralty, Captain William-Powlett and Mr Jock Anderson of the anti-submarine school, and several others visit us in Ottawa and they all seem pleased with what is going on. A few days ago I had a letter from the Navy Officer in Halifax indicating that the CD [Coastal Defence] equipment, which we built and installed in Halifax in 1940 – before many of the service officers on this side had any appreciation of what RDF was – has paid handsome dividends in the last two months. Apparently, in its purely secondary role, it prevented the loss of two vessels which were headed for a rocky coast in dense fog, and it located and discovered two bomber planes which had been lost over the Atlantic and returned them safely to their bases. Altogether it is estimated that this one set has saved the country five million dollars in two months. I took occasion to send this information to Mr Ilsley with the indication that this one set, which represents a small fraction of the work we have done in one of the sections of one of the divisions, has in two months paid back all the money which was spent on the Research Council in five years prior to the outbreak of war.

Dr John Henderson has gone, with our consent, to the Air Force on operational research. He has taken a commission and it will be his duty to see that all the many RDF equipments, both airborne and on the ground, are thoroughly understood and used by the fighting forces. I feel that you will agree with my contention that the essential objective is to have any equipment which we develop used effectively in active operations, and if this is not done then there has been no real success. I have consequently taken the viewpoint that any of our officers who can be used most effectively in operations should be permitted to go and I look for a steady drift of a limited number of our workers from the research laboratories, through development and industry, to operational research and operation in the field. I think that Henderson with his particular abilities will be of great service to the RCAF. He will, of course, maintain his connection with our laboratories and will be free to utilize our facilities, and we will be free to use him in a consulting capacity and as a liaison with the operations.

As you can imagine, we are getting cramped for space, and staff is becoming difficult to procure. To meet the space difficulties partially, we are building one-storey structures over the museums in the inside courts. I am afraid they will be a little warm in the summertime but they do give additional space which is much needed. Staff is getting more difficult to obtain and the amorphous-like policy on manpower that is still in existence in Canada does not help matters. At the council I think we are all looking forward to the day when there will be a clear-cut policy and some strong direction and control exercised over our manpower. As you can imagine, there are large numbers of scientific and technical people who are held under cover in relatively unimportant positions in government and industry and in the universities. I don't think there would be any particular resistance if someone had the authority and strength to give orders, but this philosophy of running a country by negative compulsion I am afraid is not effective in war.

I was down to Washington two weeks ago and had an interesting conference with Dr Vannevar Bush. They have followed the suggestion which you made on your recent visit and now have a three-man committee operating on a very high level, that is reporting directly to the president. It is called the Joint Committee on New Weapons. The committee consists of Dr Bush representing civilian, scientific and industrial establishments, Admiral Leighy representing the Navy, and General Moses representing the Army. This committee has no administrative or executive authority but apparently has the decision as to what developments should and should not be got on with, and will also have the power to order the services to agree on certain equipment and to concentrate their efforts on developments which it is judged are urgent and promising. I also had a conference with Dr Tolman of California, who is head of the NDRC Section on Ordnance Equipment. He is quite interested in what we are doing in Canada and is not only willing but most anxious to co-operate in every way, and I feel that any projects or studies which we wish done but which are beyond our capabilities, Tolman's group would be glad to undertake.

My wife joins me in sending best wishes to Mrs McNaughton and yourself.

Yours sincerely

C.J. MACKENZIE

HQ First Canadian Army
6 August 1942

Dear Dean Mackenzie:

In the stress of all the business of setting up the organization of First Canadian Army and other matters, I am afraid that I have shamefully neglected my correspondence with you, for which I do most sincerely apologize for I find that I have three letters unanswered, yours of 18 May, 23 June, and 14 July 1942.

Taking these in order:

Letter of 18 May:

1. I am glad to hear that an explosives laboratory is to be instituted at the National Research Council and it may be you can undertake to find the solution of a problem I put to Ritchie Donald and Col Harris some days ago, on which Donald will take all available information back with him to Canada. In order to increase the muzzle velocities of our new guns without having to provide excessively large chamber capacities, I would like to raise the permissible chamber pressure from about 28 tons per square inch to, say, 50. This means, I think, a new kind of propellant, for existing types will either not give the loading density needed, or they tend to detonate at the higher pressure. So what we need to do is to find some new chemical compound for use as a propellant; it should be unaffected by moisture and should have the smallest possible temperature coefficient. If the search for such a propellant is successful, it will open an easier road to a practical high-velocity gun than the conical bores we have been considering.

2. It is most satisfactory to note that all goes well with the development of Suffield. I am certain that chemical warfare will be used by the enemy on a

large scale, when the particular circumstances suit, and for this reason we must be on the alert against all new forms of gas and we must put ourselves in a position to retaliate with even greater effect. I am looking forward to seeing Maass about this when he arrives over here in the near future.

3. I have heard of the assistance given by Parkin and Klein to Geoffrey Pike and his special mission. This help was much appreciated by the authorities here, and I believe the matter is now going forward.

4. So far, we have only the one GL set here, and it is nearly worn out on training. We do wish the deliveries of the production models would be expedited. We are ready to put them into action the moment they arrive.

5. As regards the presidency of the National Research Council, what I would really like is that this should now go to you and I made suggestions to this effect when I was in Ottawa. If the proposal is put to you, I do hope you will accept; otherwise, it would be best to leave it to the initiative of the government.

Letter of 23 June:

6. I am glad to hear that some practical result is coming out of the cathode-ray direction finder and that some hundreds are being manufactured for the RCN and the RCAF. There is a potential use for this gear in our Special Intercepting Wireless Section and I would like to have a sample or two for experimental purposes, if it can be arranged.

Letter of 14 July:

7. I have referred to Klein's work on Geoffrey Pike's proposal in paragraph three above. I would add that this whole project is being placed on a high-priority level and Kenneth Stuart will be taking back further particulars with him.

8. Howlett knows our requirements for development of a multi-camera mount for taking line-overlap air photographs for mapping. We now plan to put this into the Mosquito light bomber, and outline specifications have been sent to Stedman through RCAF channels. The project is most important for us and I hope the experimental work will be given high priority.

9. As regards the Army Development Board, our most urgent needs are set forth in my cable GS 2016 dated 28 July 1942 to the MGO, with copies to you and Carmichael. These proposals are given there in order of priority. As regards the sight for the 20 mm, we have information from Kerrison which is additional to that taken out by Macrae. Morrison is going into the details and will take the latest information with him to Canada, so that Kerrison's new sight may be considered along with the MIT Gyro and the German FV 41.

As regards the gun itself, we do not mind whether we have the new Inglis, the Oerlikon, or the Hispano-Suiza. We want whichever one we can have quickest, for it is most urgent that we be given a thousand or more at the earliest practical date.

10. As regards projectile design for armour piercing, I would particularly like to see research work go on with a tungsten-tipped lead core in a magnesium-streamlined body, the tungsten-carbide tip to be made like an impulse turbine to ensure that the full momentum of the heavy lead core is expended in pressure forward and not used up in losses. Macrae has a rough outline of my proposals.

11. Congratulations to the National Research Council on the results achieved with CRDF at Halifax. It is indeed gratifying to know that substantial returns for our expenditures of time and money are now forthcoming.

12. I had a line from [J.T.] Henderson on his taking up his appointment with the RCAF to look after their RDF. He should do well and I think the experience will be useful, both to him and to the council. I do hope he keeps contact with our laboratories and that he will return to us later on.

13. As regards the employment of competent staffs in adequate numbers on research, the more I see of things here, the more I am certain of the message I tried to give Canada last winter that we must do our own development of new weapons and equipments. This should have first priority above production and everything must give way to this imperative need.

14. Please remember me to Dr Vannevar Bush when you see him. I enjoyed my talks with him in Washington and I am glad to see the result in

the establishment of the committee on new weapons, with which I hope Canada will have the closest possible liaison.

I appreciate your kind reference to Ian. We have had no news whatever of him since he took off on 22 June to bomb Germany, so we are still hopeful.

Things go on here much as usual – regular training to the point that the men are kept fit in all respects – steady development of our new units and formations – constant experimenting with new devices and techniques, etc. At the moment, we have CGS [Chief of the General Staff] and AG Canada [Adjutant General] with us, which is most useful, as they will carry home our views on many matters which cannot be fully explained and reconciled in cables.

My wife is well and joins me in kindest regards to yourself and Mrs Mackenzie.

Very sincerely yours

A.G.L. McNaughton
Lieutenant-General
General Officer Commanding-in-Chief
First Canadian Army Overseas

Ottawa
1 September 1942

Dear General McNaughton:

I have intended writing to you for some time to give you a complete account of what has been happening. Things have been moving rapidly and I was waiting for some of them to crystallize before bothering you. However, I am writing this note as I would like the following information to get to you by the plane which leaves within two hours.

The Army Technical Development Board is becoming extraordinarily active and I think that you would be pleased with the developments. Major Hahn of the John Inglis Company agreed to take over the job of director general and to devote his full time to the work. As you know, Colonel Harkness did some early work but was not able to get away from his company for more than half time.

Major Hahn and I have been working intimately on the proposals and we have visited many plants and interviewed all the directors in the MGO's office, etc. I am quite optimistic and think we have finally got an excellent arrangement.

Major Hahn is extremely keen about the matter and feels as intensely as you do about the urgency and need of getting on with developments here, and he is a man who will not be blocked. He is much impressed with the work which the council can do and is determined that there shall be the closest co-ordination of our efforts in all military fields.

Major Hahn is working night and day at the job. He is going to Washington this week to see the situation there and then is taking the first available plane to England. I am writing this letter as I thought you might be interested to know my opinion of what is happening before Major Hahn sees you in England. We were in Toronto on Friday and saw the first shots fired in his new 20 mm automatic. Rose is presently in the United States getting all information on sights available. Hahn insists that a time deadline shall be set on everything that is being done.

I hope that you will feel as I do that the spirit which you came to Canada last February to instil into the Army development work is being achieved. I will write a more detailed letter later but I want this to catch the plane today.

With kindest personal regards.

Your sincerely

C.J. MACKENZIE

PS – I am enclosing a report which Major Hahn has made and which sets forth his summing-up of the present situation and his ideas as to future organization.

Ottawa
21 September 1942

Dear General McNaughton:

This will be one of my general news-letters as many things have been happening recently and I want to be able to bring you up to date on the most recent developments. While I enjoy receiving your letters I would like you to feel that my letters are simply to keep you informed and do not need any acknowledgement. I realize what a great strain there must be on your time and energies.

I have just finished a meeting of the Research Council and the War Technical and Scientific Development Committee. You will be interested to hear that we have at last got clear of the fire-hazards laboratory by passing it over to the CESA as you originally planned.

The greatest activities recently have been, as you know, in connection with the Army Technical Development Board, and no doubt by the time you have received this letter Major Hahn will have given you more detailed information. I think the arrangement is going to work out well and is satisfactory as far as the council is concerned. We now have a voice in all army development plans on the highest level and the tasks which are assigned to us will be within our competence; our facilities in obtaining not only financial support, but also the support of industry and other branches of the service, will be made much easier.

At the last meeting of the Army Technical Development Board a grant of $450,000 was made for a pilot plant for high explosives and propellants, to be designed and built under the auspices of the National Research Council. After a great deal of study and a visit to the United States it was decided that these plants should be built at Valcartier where a proving ground and other ballistics facilities are available. I think that, from the standpoint of post-war work, the decision was a wise one.

Rose is at the present time busy on a gun sight for the John Inglis 20 mm automatic and we are organizing into a group workers such as R.H. Field, Rose, Klein, etc., who are interested in armament and ballistics problems. I have taken on my staff Dr W.L. Webster who, as you know, is the son of Dr Webster of Shediac and who was at one time with the Ministry of Supply in England and latterly has been secretary of the British Central Scientific Office in Washington. He is knowledgeable on scientific and technical developments in connection with the Army and I propose to use him as a personal assistant. He will act as secretary to the ballistics groups and form a liaison with Hahn's organization at Defence Headquarters.

The deliveries of GL sets, as you say, have been disappointing but we have done everything we can to hurry the matter along. The delay, I think, is caused by the time required to tune up the sets as they are finished. We told REL [Research Enterprises Limited] months ago that, in our opinion, that part of the operation was a major one as it had taken us about six weeks, with a highly expert staff of a dozen or so, to tune up our own; that if they were contemplating one GL a day we foresaw difficulties, and I think they are experiencing those difficulties now. However, we have maintained a number of our personnel at their plant for weeks now and are giving them every assistance. It looks as if the dam would burst at any moment and the GLS start to flow out in reasonable quantities.

We had a meeting of our RDF committee this afternoon and Mr Hackbusch has given me the following information which may be of interest to you. GL sets 1, 2, 4, and 5 were delivered to the Canadian Army in June, July, and August. Number 3 was shipped to England from REL on August 13 and sets number 6, 7, and 8 were shipped from REL on August 30, September 15, and September 17; but Mr Hackbusch claims that these sets have been standing at the siding at Long Point, near Montreal, since about that date, apparently awaiting facilities for shipment. Set number 9 was turned out of REL today and sets 10, 11, 12, and 13 will be finished this week and ready for shipment to England on US account. Set numer 14 comes to Canada and sets 15 and 16 will go to England and will be ready by the last week in September. According to Mr Hackbush, the definite allocation of the sets from 17 on has not yet been made but he promises 22 sets finished in October, 48 in November, and 60 in December. Whether or not REL will live up to this promise I do not know.

At the meeting today the problem of shipping was raised and apparently, if the decision to send them over only in NA convoys is maintained, there will be great difficulty in getting the material to England in quantity. The committee decided to recommend that trailer number 1, which is really the most intricate and secret component, should be sent on NA convoys under security guard, but that the trucks, diesel, and number 2 trailer should be permitted to go by ordinary freighter even at the risk of loss.

Howlett is getting along reasonably well with his committee on air photography; the Mosquito light bomber is to be delivered at Test and Development Flight at Rockcliffe within the next few days and multi-camera mounts are under construction. Howlett thoroughly appreciates the high priority which you give this project and has done everything to push things along, but it took some time before we could get the necessary action.

With regard to research on tungsten-carbide-tipped cores, we are having difficulty in Canada because it is almost impossible to obtain any tungsten carbide beyond that required for machine tools. We had a meeting recently in my office at which General Macrae presided and the metals controller told us he saw no immediate hopes for us obtaining any considerable amount of tungsten carbide.

Sir Frank Smith called on us for a few minutes last week. He spent an afternoon at REL and the best part of a day in Ottawa. I think he was surprised at what we were doing in Canada and particularly in the optical glass and radio fields, as he has always been of the opinion, I take it, that nothing at all intricate can be made in this country. As with a great many of the pre-war industrialists in England, one cannot help feeling that the wish is father to the thought.

You will be pleased to know that Klein has been able to be of some use to Geoffrey Pike and his knowledge of snow conditions has been put to good use in design details.

I think I told you before that the Signals Branch of the Army is building a laboratory on the National Research Council property. You will be interested to hear that the plans have already been drawn and approved and I expect the building will be started shortly.

Geoffrey Hill is enjoying his work in Canada and is fitting into our organization well. He is popular and gets on well with everyone. At the present time he is making a trip to the Pacific coast to visit the various aeronautical establishments. We are going to do some experimental work on his pterodactyl tailless plane but whether or not we can get a half-scale model built in Canada is something which we will have to consider.

Maass returned safely to Canada after a rather eventful trip and is busy at his duties in connection with chemical warfare. I telephoned Vannevar Bush and made an appointment for Maass to see him in Washington to disclose the information which you suggested he should give to Bush.

You will be interested to know that I have negotiations under way which may solve the Canadian Refractories contract.* According to our figures we have spent, over and above receipts, about $110,000 on this project. At the present time the royalty payments are satisfactory and this year we will receive about $23,000, but under the agreement we will still be paying out $13,000 so that even at the present satisfactory rate it would take us about ten years to liquidate our indebtedness; when the war is over, the royalty payments will undoubtedly fall off badly and I doubt whether under the present arrangement we could ever break even. I suggested to Pitt the other day that with the present favourable earnings of the company he should pay us up entirely. If he would make a cash settlement for the total indebtedness we would cancel the agreement and the future royalty payments, and we would then enter into a new agree-

---

*Canadian Refractories Limited had been founded on NRC research on magnesite. Dr H.M. Tory, president of the NRC from 1928 to 1935, was fond of pointing out that this single item of research had repaid to the country far more than the entire cost of the NRC from its beginning to date.

ment on a straight Mellon Institute basis whereby his company would pay the actual expenses plus an overhead for all work done. I also indicated that in our opinion a large percentage of the work done in the laboratory was of a plant-control nature and would be better done at their plant than in our building. Pitt agreed to the general proposals and said that he would put it before his directors. He subsequently told me that Mr Kilbourn, his president, had agreed and that he thought he could reach a settlement at an early date. I think if we could get out of this agreement in this satisfactory way and with the best of feelings on the part of everyone that we would be lucky, and I hope that you agree with me.

We are arriving at the point now at the Research Council where we have more problems than we can undertake. We have just completed an internal survey to eliminate everything that is not of real urgency in connection with the war, and we will have to regulate our activities now on a strict basis of priorities.

I can well realize what a strain the Dieppe expedition must have been on you and, while the losses are apparently appreciable, I think everyone in Canada is proud of the way the troops carried on, which is a reflection of the sound training which they have had.

With regard to the presidency of the National Research Council, I would much prefer that it remain as it is until you return, as I value the opportunity of serving as your substitute much more than I would appreciate the direct appointment; so that if you agree, as far as I am concerned I would like to leave it as it is.

My wife joins me in kindest regards to Mrs McNaughton and yourself.

Sincerely yours

C.J. MACKENZIE

Ottawa
2 January 1943

Dear General McNaughton:

I am seizing this opportunity at the beginning of the year to write you a brief news-letter. I do not know whether most other departments are experiencing the same thing, but the frantic period seems to be getting over in the council. I suppose it is because we have things better organized and most of our groups are working steadily on problems, with the result that there are fewer crises and urgent undertakings to deal with.

For the first time since I came to Ottawa, I have been able to find a few hours to do some of the things I have always wanted to do since I came here. I have been able to move around a bit and will do more in the future, as that side of my existence here had to be very much curtailed in the early days. I am beginning to feel now for the first time that the institution could run a month or six weeks on its own and I am planning to go to England after the March meeting of the council. There is no specific reason for my going, but I hope that you feel as I do that it would be a useful trip and would enable me to make personal contacts and see the various institutions in England in operation. I have wanted to do this for the last two years, but always felt that it was my duty to remain pretty close to the job here in the days when policy had to be determined, negotiations carried on, and decisions of far-reaching importance made almost daily.

There have been a number of interesting developments since I last wrote. Manske has gone to the Dominion Rubber Company to organize and head a research laboratory. Mr Paul Jones, the president, interviewed me and told me that while they had large laboratories in the United States, he felt that all the Canadian companies should have research laboratories in Canada, and with that policy I heartily agree. He asked me if he could approach some member of our staff to head his laboratory and I gave him permission to approach Manske. They are being generous in the salary schedule and are paying Manske fifteen thousand dollars a year. My own feeling is that it would be highly desirable if all of the large companies, including the subsidiaries of the large electrical and chemical industries, would, after the war, organize laboratories in Canada, even if they were branch laboratories, and I think it would be in the interest of the council if the heads of such laboratories were drawn from our staff.

The plans for the explosives pilot plant which we are to build are well under way. I think I told you before that we had decided to build at Valcartier near the filling plant and Brigadier Theriault has been helpful. Incidentally, he was most anxious that I should convey to you his best wishes and he was, I think, most anxious also that you should know that he was helping us in every way possible. I have the feeling that with the explosives pilot plant, the filling plant, and the ballistics proving ground at Valcartier, and the gun plant at Sorel, there might develop a valuable centre of scientific interest in that part of Quebec which could be carried on after the war.

The highly secret BW unit at Grosse Isle is well under way. It is a co-operative enterprise between the United States and Canada and for administration is under Dr Maass as director of Chemical Warfare. This is another of the many projects which Sir Frederick was keen about in the early days of the war. When I think of all of the projects which Sir Frederick started and observe now how many of them have proven eminently successful, the stark tragedy of his early death bears heavily upon me.

We have recently organized the explosives research on a comprehensive basis. We have a main explosives committee and three subcommittees, one covering the pilot plant at Valcartier, which I have just referred to; another operating the Explosives Testing Laboratory on the Montreal Road site and a third subcommittee which directs extra-mural work. This latter subcommittee under Professor Wright, University of Toronto, has now some fifty projects under way at the different universities, and I think the work being done in Canada on explosives will prove to be a bright spot in our many achievements. We have also tried to organize all of the ballistic work which is going on in Canada in the various departments. I persuaded Major-General Macrae to take the chairmanship of the main committee and there are representatives from the Department of Munitions and Supply, Army Engineering Design Branch, Inspection Board, the Departments of National Defence, Mines and Resources, and the National Research Council.

As you will realize, the ballistics field is large and intricate, and the contacts with the services are so intimate that it is difficult to draw a border line between development, research, and production. However, we hope that the co-operative group which we have formed will serve a useful purpose.

The Radio Section is continuing its excellent work, but production at REL has not been so satisfactory. I am afraid that Colonel Phillips has not had the best help in his assistants as Hackbusch is an energetic man who, in addition to not being highly experienced as an industrialist, is a grand buck-passer and is continually blaming everybody, including ourselves, the services, the Inspection Board, and in fact everyone he comes in contact with for the faults which are really his own. However, the council has been particularly careful to avoid any criticism at all and has maintained excellent arrangements with Phillips and most of his crowd. I have never said what I have just written to anyone else and I hope that you will not quote me, as we have to work so intimately with the organization that we are leaning over backwards to prevent any friction while there is any possibility of improving matters. We have one interest, and one interest only, and that is to do everything we can to assist in getting out equipment; Colonel Wallace and I have both insisted that no word of criticism, however justified, should come out of the National Research Council while we are engaged in this vital work.

Major Hahn is being active in the Army Technical Development Board and is a first-class organizer. He has organized the various directorates of the MGO's office as far as attention to new weapons and equipment is concerned; by instituting a system of reports he keeps them all on their toes and is doing a useful job. We in the council are co-operating to the fullest extent with all of the directorates and I think the procedure which we adopted is the wisest one. At one time Major Hahn wanted to make up a folder in one of his report books covering the work of the National Research Council. I objected to that as all of the other agencies reporting were directorates of the Department of National Defence and there is so much work going on in the Research Council which could not be reported that if we simply detached a few of the things, like gun sights, explosives plants, proximity fuses, etc., it would give an imperfect picture of what we are doing. Also, the types of reports which the other directorates are concerned with are not similar to ours. I convinced him that the proper procedure as far as he was concerned was to have the reports of his directorates include reference to the Research Council when research work was being done on a project by the council and we in turn would report through the directorates concerned. The situation is something like this: When a directorate decides to undertake a project which is accepted by the ATDB, a decision is made as to how the work will be carried on, and if the Research Council can be of any assistance it is named as a co-operating agency and we work directly with them. The directorate details an officer and we designate one of our scientists who will together be responsible for carrying out the research project and seeing to it that the work goes on effectively and efficiently. The system is working well.

In Parkin's division there is much activity. Klein was useful with the project with which Geoffrey Pike was concerned and the equipment, as you know, has satisfactorily passed field trials. The work on plastic plywoods has been extraordinarily useful and we are now making Harvard fuselages and other aircraft parts. Geoffrey Hill, who has just returned from England, is interested in his tailless aircraft and pleased with the wind-tunnel work which Green and his staff have done in that connection. Hill is trying to induce the British to send over a team of designers to work actively on his proposals, and if we could have such a team located at the Research Council I think it would give considerable stimulation to our aeronautical people.

The Army Signals Laboratory on the Montreal Road site is getting along well and will be completed by spring. The new hydraulic laboratory which will also house the fire-testing laboratory is under way. The new engine stand and icing tunnel and the addition to the power plant are being rushed to completion. I have thought from time to time of trying to get the high-tension laboratory built on the Montreal Road site, on the basis that it will be much needed after the war. I think I could find the money quite easily, but there is such a definite shortage of building materials here in Canada at the moment that the Department of Munitions and Supply is only granting permits for buildings when the need is very urgent.

You will also be interested to know that we have reached a final agreement with Canadian Refractories and before the end of the year they will pay us a lump sum in the neighbourhood of $110,000, which will put us in the position of being able to say that all of the most valuable work which has been done in establishing this Canadian industry has been done without the expenditure of one cent of public money. It is a position which I do not think anyone here thought could be obtained. I am even more pleased that the agreement has been reached in the most friendly spirit and apparently is completely satisfactory to everyone.

After a delay of six or seven months from the time when the authorizing Order in Council was put through, we were finally able to obtain war supplements for certain members of our technical staff. As you know, we laboured under most unjust handicaps in that there was a freezing order making it impossible to increase the salary of any member of our permanent staff, but at the same time the staffs in the war units and in industry were paid sometimes two to three times as much for the same work. In addition, many of our technical staff who were in the services got rapid promotion, and there were many instances where the head of our laboratory was being paid twenty-seven or twenty-eight hundred dollars and his immediate juniors would be taken into industry at almost double that figure. However, we have some relief now and I have been able to get moderate adjustments in the salaries of our permanent technical staff who have assumed additional responsibilities in connection with the war.

I have tried for months to get the Research Council accepted as a war unit, which it is in fact as there is practically no peace-time work going on and our staff has increased from three hundred to thirteen hundred; but I cannot get it through our friend Ronson although, as I have pointed out to him, it would not cost the government a nickel and it is these irritating things that cause inefficiency.

I have also failed completely in my efforts to get protection for the senior people travelling to England. At present, as you know, the situation is that members of our staff, if killed or disabled in an aeroplane crash going across the Atlantic or by bombs or gun-fire in England, would have the same pension protection as a lieutenant in the Army. This, of course, is all right for our junior men, but for the senior people with wives and small families it is most inadequate and most unjust. But apparently nothing can be done about it.

On the whole, however, I think the National Research Council is used very well, and I was most amazed on New Year's Day at a conversation I had at the club after the Governor General's Levee. I was sitting with two senior cabinet ministers, one of whom is on the Treasury Board, and the other the minister of National Defence, and was most surprised to hear them say they not only thought that the Research Council was doing an excellent job in the war, but, due to the nature of our work and the character of our organization, we should have a special type of set-up which would relieve us from many of the annoying and troublesome regulations which cover the ordinary public service. That, I think you will agree, would be a most desirable end, and I hope that after the war the government can be made to see the necessity for amending the Research Council Act.

As you have perhaps heard, we have had in Ottawa one of the worst storms for thirty years. The street railway has been dislocated and for three days there have been no cars running anywhere in the system. Outside of delays and loss of time in getting about, however, there has been no real hardship.

I have just received a report of the field trials of the CRDF equipment which is being made for the Navy. As this is really your scientific child, I am sending a full copy of the report which I think should give you some satisfaction.

I was down to Washington a few days ago and had lunch with Dr Bush and dinner with President Conant of Harvard, both of whom are good friends of ours and give us excellent co-operation. Dr Bush particularly asked me to give you his regards when I wrote and I would like to tell you how kind they have been. The three key men in the scientific hierarchy in Washington seem to be Dr Bush, President Conant of Harvard, and Dr Compton, president of MIT. Of course there are many other active and able scientists, but these three men are in key positions and they are all most kind and generous to us in all our contacts.

My wife joins me in sending to Mrs McNaughton and yourself the compliments of the season and our very best wishes that our hopes for the New Year will be fulfilled.

Sincerely yours

C.J. MACKENZIE

Ottawa
28 September 1943

Dear General McNaughton:

I must apologize for not having written you since coming back to Canada,* but I was very busy immediately after getting back and the days slip by so quickly that one does not realize that weeks are turning into months. However, with the many visitors who pass to and fro these days, you have no doubt followed roughly the work the council is doing.

I think the most important general observation is that our programs have become adjusted to the course of the war. While in the early days of '39 and '40 we were perhaps in the best position to anticipate needs and initiate projects while the services were becoming organized, gaining experience and equipping thoroughly with technical staff, we feel that that period is over and now we are working chiefly on direct demands from the various service staffs, which in turn are indicated by the users in the field. For the same reason we have extended our actual contact with the services and are working closely with their technical officers and organizations, such as the Army Technical Development Board, and operational-research groups. We have given personnel to the services and industry wherever it seemed helpful, and have allowed our staff to go wherever their abilities could be most effectively used in the main object of winning the war.

As you know, the Air Force and Navy both have well-organized operational-research groups, who are functioning with the operational forces on the Atlantic and Pacific coasts. Many of our staff have joined these groups and all of the civilians are on our pay-roll and seconded to the services, so that our tie-in is very good.

As you also know, there is a proposal now that Dr Rose should be appointed scientific adviser to Army Headquarters in Ottawa. If that proposal works out it seems to me much benefit should be forthcoming. I have always felt that the type of Army operational unit that is effective overseas would not necessarily be effective in Canada; but I do feel that if

---

*Mackenzie was in England during May and June of 1943.

we can get a scientific unit which will be able to advise the General Staff on the planning and carrying out of trials, the testing of equipment, and the many other activities where scientific techniques are useful, a contribution might be made. There will be many immediate problems; for instance, the Army is undertaking extensive cold-weather trials this winter and it seems to me that scientists should be of great value in advising on the layout and conduct of programs and tests to obtain the information that the General Staff requires.

Dr W.H. Cook has just returned from a trip to South America where he went as the only scientific member, from our side, of a joint UK-US commission on foods. As would be expected, he did a good job and has come back full of useful information and ideas.

The Chemistry Division is busy on a wide program of testing and consulting for the Army, and the work that is being done on protective clothing for all services is notable.

Dr Pidgeon has accepted the professorship of Metallurgy at the University of Toronto and I gave him the council's blessing in his new venture.

The Physics and Mechanical Engineering Divisions are both busy on programs along lines with which you are familiar.

I spent two days at the Quebec Conference, to which I was invited by the British delegates, to consider Habakkuk and various other scientific matters which were being dealt with by the joint groups. I do not think that Habakkuk will become an actual reality but Mr Churchill has been pressing the matter vigorously; while in Washington, he turned his guns on the American Navy with the result that, after much resistance, they finally agreed to make a serious study of the problem and we are to give them the results of the work done in Canada.

With the closer development of co-operation between the United Kingdom and the United States, I have been called to Washington many times to attend joint conferences.* We are on a most friendly basis with both the Americans and Britishers and I think that I have been useful to the two parties in composing differences of outlook and opinion.

As you know, our Biology Division has been interested in the industrial utilization of agricultural products and we have already done some con-

*Subsequent to the Quebec Conference of August 1943, at which Churchill, Roosevelt and Mackenzie King committed their three nations to full co-ordination of nuclear research, C.J. Mackenzie was appointed the Canadian member of an international three-man technical committee charged with correlating the policy decisions of the three governments.

structive work in connection with the production of butadiene by the fermentation of wheat. The Polymer Corporation, which is entrusted with the construction of the large synthetic-rubber company in Canada, is friendly to us, and I had a meeting with the president, Mr Berkinshaw, a few weeks ago; he is suggesting that we undertake a more extensive research program in connection with the whole synthetic-rubber project.

As you probably know, the political situation in Canada is full of interest and activity. The government lost four by-elections in a row and are quite concerned about their future. A convention of the Liberal party is meeting in Ottawa at the present time and all sorts of rumours are flying about. There is much dissatisfaction throughout the country and many pressure groups are working to break the price ceiling and other restraints which I feel are of fundamental importance but are not politically profitable. I understand that some of the party are in favour of an immediate election, but my guess is there will not be one until next year; but it is not unreasonable to expect some changes in policy before that time.

I had an embarrassing few hours in the dying days of the last session. You will recall that before the war you had asked Dr Newton to consider the proposal of having a branch of the Research Council established in the western provinces to study the particular problems of that area, but at the outbreak of war we felt it was impossible to go on with such a proposal. However, the Biology Division has been doing a lot of quiet work and we have been laying plans. Last winter there was a great deal of agitation in Western Canada for a western laboratory, probably because the prairie provinces have not participated in the general war industrial developments in the same way as have the other provinces. At any rate, just before the House prorogued, Mr [Rt Hon James] Gardiner telegraphed from western Canada and insisted that an item of five hundred thousand dollars be placed in the supplementary estimates for the construction and operation of a western laboratory to study the industrial uses of agricultural products. The Treasury Board, I feel, were not keen to have the project undertaken in that way, although they were generally in favour of doing something. I was summoned to a hurried meeting of Treasury Board. The Agriculture people were also there. I told them that we had been studying the project for a long time as it was in our field of activity, but that in keeping with the request of the Treasury Board for restriction of all strictly peace-time activities, we had deferred action and we did not believe that a project of such magnitude and ultimate consequences should be undertaken without serious consideration. The result was that the amount was cut down to $150,000 with the rider that no expenditure could be made without the consent of the National Research Council, from which you will see our standing at Treasury Board is fairly good. However, it clearly indicated that we would have to become active and I have now formed a committee, headed by Dr Newton and made up of western membership, which is to meet in Saskatoon in November to study the entire subject. It is a delicate matter and requires tact and wisdom.

You probably know that there have been various committees concerning themselves with post-war activities for some time, but up to the present I have taken the stand that we were so involved in ad hoc and immediate war problems that the time was not ripe for consideration of post-war activities. I have now come to the conclusion that we must do something, at least in a tentative way, although I do not propose to do it publicly or divert any considerable portion of council energy to that field. On the other hand, there can be no question that the reason the Research Council was able to become useful immediately on the outbreak of war and to make the contribution it did in the early stages was because you had been doing careful planning for the war before it broke out and that facilities were available when needed. In the same way I feel there will be innumerable problems when the war is over and that we should now do some thinking and have plans ready, so that we will be prepared not only to recommend constructive measures, but to criticize ill-conceived programs prompted by political expediency. For that reason I have asked the Review Committee this year to take as its major activity consideration of the post-war position of the council. Accordingly, last week we had a preliminary discussion for two days at which the directors and their section heads were invited to lay before the committee, in a preliminary way, their ideas on post-war activities. It was an interesting meeting and Mr J.S. Duncan, who has been appointed a member of our council, told me afterwards that he had been a member of Principal James's Committee on Reconstruction for a year and had attended numerous meetings, but that in one forenoon at our Review Committee he heard more interesting and constructive suggestions than he had in the past year.

There are other broader issues which are giving me some concern, particularly as my connection with the council is of a temporary nature, and for that reason I would like your advice. The picture in brief is that the work of the Research Council during the war years has created a favourable impression and the government as a whole is kindly disposed to us and rather favours all scientific work being done under our auspices. The associate-committee machinery has worked extraordinarily well and the advantages of working under our auspices have become appreciated not only by the services but by scientific institutions in other government departments. For instance, in connection with Navy problems which are essentially service projects, such as the smoke-laying craft that is being developed for exercises in the immediate future, the ATDB accepted my proposal of an associate committee as the mechanism most suitable for prompt work. An associate committee was set up with Kuhring as chairman and the only civilian member. The money was granted to us by ATDB and the work is being done by Kuhring, Casey Baldwin at Baddeck, and the chemical-warfare people at Suffield in an incredibly short time – I just witnessed a demonstration this morning, with Kuhring piloting the craft at fifty miles per hour on the Ottawa River.* The Air Force in their medical work are equally impressed, and it is getting to the point with the Mines and Resources people where Timm of the Bureau of Mines and Roy Cameron and McElhanney, etc., discuss a great many of their problems with us, and Dr [Charles] Camsell has made a point of asking us to examine all submissions that he is presenting for increased facilities, etc., as he feels that our support is almost necessary.

Owing to all this there is growing up a general feeling that what we should have in Canada is something like the DSIR [Department of Scientific and Industrial Research] in England – a department of government without other administrative responsibilities which would generally administer all the scientific laboratories and agencies of government and be responsible for the general over-all co-ordination and sponsoring of national projects. The system in my view would be simply an extension of the present Research Council system which, as you well know, has two main functions: first, the stimulating of research by scholarships, grants-in-aid to universities, and the organizing and co-ordinating of broad projects by the mechanism of associate committees, and secondly the detailed administration of our own research laboratories. The same end could be reached in two ways: either a department could be organized as outlined above, or all of the scientific laboratories could be placed under the jurisdiction of the Research Council. The people who favour the first scheme suggest that it might be difficult to detach the scientific laboratories of the other departments for absorption into the Research Council, and the second argument is that the ministerial contact at present is a fortuitous one and that Trade and

---

*This was one of the first successful uses of the hydrofoil, capable of operating in heavy seas – nine- or ten-foot waves – at 40 mph.

Commerce is not the obvious department for such an organization as ours has grown into.

The above is a general picture of what is running through some minds, and while I hesitate to suggest that you divert any of your energies from your present onerous and immediate responsibilities, I do not feel it would be right for me to discuss seriously with responsible people future plans of this nature without your consent and general agreement. While I am not one of those who is over-optimistic about the end of the war, I do know that with the present political situation in Canada, plans are being discussed and one never knows when suggestions given or seeds planted will bear fruit. There are some who feel quite strongly that if an immediate election were called, the chances are that the CCF might be returned, if not with a majority at least as the largest group. When one considers the chaos that would exist while inexperienced people were finding their feet, one cannot help toying with the idea that it might be better to get our future settled while a government is in power that understands generally our needs.

I am always glad to hear from our many mutual friends that you are well and that the results of your years of brilliant and unselfish efforts are beginning to appear in action. We were all thrilled at the performance of the First Division in Sicily, and I know you must feel a great deal of pride in their achievements.

My wife joins me in sending kindest remembrances to Mrs McNaughton and yourself.

Yours sincerely

C.J. MACKENZIE

C.J. MACKENZIE

Epilogue

Early Monday morning, 7 May 1945, a few miles out of Sioux Lookout, Ontario, a train carrying three hundred war brides and seventy babies went off the track. The train on which I was travelling was held up six hours. A rumour, which proved correct, came through about 9 AM, saying that the war was over in Europe. Passenger reaction seemed restrained. I arrived in Winnipeg at 4.30 PM and, being too late for my appointment with the chairman of the Regional Advisory Council of the Department of Reconstruction, had time to look around. The day was dull, the wind raw. There apparently had been some kind of celebration in the morning but already the only evidence of this was litter blowing in the wind on deserted streets.

What a contrast with the spontaneous and joyous outburst of 11 November 1918; then, 'the war to end all wars' had been won. On this day there was no such euphoric rejoicing. Relief, yes; but now we knew that military victory does not guarantee permanent peace, and that many hoped-for national benefits often turn to liabilities. Scientific development fortunately does not suffer such a melancholy fate.

In six years of war, foundations had been laid in Canada for a sound scientific and technological structure, the essentials for modern industrial competence. In 1939, apart from scientific activities concerning national resources, Canada had had little competence and no international standing in the field of 'big science.' The only establishment of any size in this category was at the National Research Council where a total staff of three hundred was spending less than a million dollars a year.

In the war years, Canada had won international respect for its competence in developing and producing complex equipment, requiring sophisticated techniques in both laboratories and industries. The National Research Council laboratory staff had increased five times – but its size alone was not large by international comparison. However, NRC was not alone. As the war went on, most of Canada's scientific manpower resources in governments, in universities, and in industry were welded into a mission-oriented, sizable group in which they associated together, often informally, but always in effective and harmonious co-operation.

Many thoughts flashed across my mind during those dull hours spent on that stalled train near Sioux Lookout (and, later, at Winnipeg) on VE day. Canadian war projects that had not been backed up by strong scientific research-and-development establishments had tended to be unsuccessful; for example, millions of dollars had been spent on army tanks that field commanders would not use in actual combat. And how terribly vulnerable our branch-plant complex had made us in certain crises, as in the radar story: by June 1940, NRC laboratories had developed prototype radar sets ready for mass production, but radar was a secret British innovation and the only industrial plants in Canada competent to undertake the job were subsidiaries of American firms. The United States was then a neutral country and British military secrets could not be disclosed to US branch factories in Canada; so the Department of Munitions and Supply had to set up a Crown corporation (Research Enterprises Limited). This factory was producing radar sets and optical glass six months before Pearl Harbor brought the Americans into the war.

One recalled our happy early associations with Polymer, another Crown corporation created to produce artificial rubber. On 4 November 1943, the president and general manager of the corporation approached NRC and said that their American wartime associates had agreed to make all their patents and licences on artificial rubber available, if Polymer Corporation would spend $250,000 on basic research and make all its findings available to the American plants. Polymer at that time had no research group and asked us if NRC could assist them in meeting the US proposal. We saw in this arrangement an excellent opportunity to undertake research, in close co-operation with a company which might well develop into an important peace-time chemical industry in Canada. The Research Council set up an Associate Committee on Artificial Rubber and arranged for a broad program of basic exploratory research in numerous university and government laboratories. This association brought us into contact with the plant, and we were also of assistance in supporting their plans for a first-class applied-research laboratory at their factory, which rounded out a competent industrial operation.

Another wartime project stood out vividly in memory as an excellent example of two things; first, the ideal path from idea to use and, second, the difficulty of attaining this ideal in peace time. Early in the war, our radar group was asked by the Royal Canadian Navy to develop a radar set for motor torpedo boats: a group of NRC scientists joined the officers of a naval craft on an actual operation and were given the requirements of range, space, size, and required rugged features. The NRC group then returned to its laboratory and produced a working prototype; in this phase, the head of the NRC group was in charge, but visitors from the Navy and REL joined the group as advisers. The prototype set was then tested under actual service conditions by the Navy; in this phase, NRC engineers were present as observers. When the Navy was satisfied as to operational characteristics, the set was taken to REL where a production engineer was in command, but staff from Navy and NRC had the duty of seeing that the procedures for mass production did not endanger the essential requirements of technical behaviour, size restriction, and ruggedness. The final result of this co-operation and joint responsibility was a set that was an immediate and outstanding success, and REL received sizable production contracts without delay.

But not all war projects were ultimately so successful. One of these was the jet engine. In 1943, NRC sent two senior aeronautical engineers to England as visitors to Air Commodore Frank Whittle's establishment, where the pioneering work on jet engines was being done. On their return, as a first step, NRC financed the building of small testing stations in Canada. Munitions and Supply then became interested and set up a Crown corporation with sizable funds to expand the work being done by council engineers. Eventually, a Canadian subsidiary of an experienced English industrial company took over the project (and the staff of Canadian scientific engineers) and, with government financial support, continued the development of one hundred per cent Canadian-designed and built jet engines. The company also built and tested successfully both military and civilian aeroplanes. This product of able Canadian scientists, engineers, and industrialists was a technological success, but foundered on the rocks of political policy decisions. If Canadian industries in peace could only be certain of customer needs and firm purchase contracts, innovation would be rather simple instead of complicated and financially hazardous.

That unhappy story was still more than a decade away, however, as I pondered on VE day. But the process of post-war reorganization was already under way.

In August of 1943, I had been invited by British officials to attend the Quebec Conference to discuss certain technical proposals concerning plans for the invasion of Europe. It became clear to me there that planning in all phases was in the final stages and, from the supply position, novel weapons or equipment that was not already in advanced prototype form would never be used in the current war. Therefore, we began to phase out research and development work on such projects and put more stress on technical support for industrial production of developed prototypes, and on seconding scientists and engineers to work on the 'operational research' being organized by the services in Canada. On the senior level, we began to give increased thought to post-war problems; active planning committees of the staff and the Honourary Council got busy, drafting reports for consideration at the March 1944 meeting of the council.

Planning studies were also under way in most government departments and agencies, and it was understood that the prime minister and his cabinet were even then busy drafting social-security and welfare legislation – and no doubt planning political strategies as well, for an early election.

As one would expect, C.D. Howe seemed to be the one cabinet minister who was really interested in and knowledgeable about the part research had played in war, and must play in the reconstruction period. In October 1943, he asked me to prepare some notes for him on the discussions and studies that were going on at NRC. The following extracts are taken from a report made to him on November 30, 1943:

Dear Mr. Howe:

As promised, I am putting down a few thoughts on the future of scientific research in Canada. ... I suggest that a greatly increased program of peace-time research must be undertaken after the war, primarily because it is in the nation's interest to do so and, secondly, because there is a growing public demand for it. ... It is interesting ... that Mr Arthur Little remarked, a few years ago, that, of the industries established on this continent during the last war [World War I], only those survived which were based on scientific research and laboratory technology. ... It is almost impossible to obtain exact figures as to the total money spent by a nation on scientific research because the word "research" is so loosely used and, also, because scientific work is normally done under so many agencies. ... Perhaps a good way is to consider the amounts spent as a percentage of the national income, but, any way gross figures are looked at, it becomes evident that Canada, if she is to maintain the position she has gained during the war, must materially increase her expenditures on scientific research. ... In 1943–4, the National Research Council will spend about six million dollars in ... its own laboratories and allied co-operative projects. ... We are using practically all the scientific personnel available in Canada and any large increase ... would not be immediately possible, but ... we should aim at maintaining, in the immediate post-war period, the present scale of activities and expand as personnel become available. ...

What of the problems to be attacked? They are literally legion: investigations to assist in the industrial development of the Dominion; [and] studies in connection with the ... general living conditions of the people. ...

While we are now manufacturing artificial rubber, and are fabricating plastics and producing a considerable line of chemicals, up to the present time very little research has been done in Canada. ... We have imported most of our scientific information and, in many cases, the chemical materials themselves. ...

In the broad field of transport ... there are an increasing number of problems in connection with air, road, and rail transportation. ...

The whole problem of cold-weather operations in northern regions is receiving a great deal of attention these days, not only in connection with flying and operation of mechanical equipment, but with general industry and living conditions. We are particularly well located in Canada to study fundamentally the mechanics of snow, ice, and the influence of low temperature on ... activities in cold regions. ...

One of the most important fields in which we have done little in Canada is that of housing in all its aspects, including properties of building material, insulation, lighting, heating, acoustics, refrigeration, planning, and economical construction. One of our greatest needs at present is for a first-class building research station. ...

Metallurgy is growing more important every day and becoming a highly scientific field, requiring the intimate co-operation of metallurgists, chemists and physicists. ... Canada ... should expand and broaden her activities in this field. ... Coupled with this, we should have in Canada a laboratory for studying ... materials from the standpoint of fundamental structure of matter. ... This would be a co-operative study by physicists, radiologists, chemists, metallurgists, and engineers. ... First a number of laboratories and institutes must be set up to fill the scientific gaps in our present facilities and, secondly, we must decide how we are going to organize and administer the system. ...

At the present time, the National Research Council has two distinct functions: (a) it administers its own research laboratories, and (b) it organizes co-operative research across Canada. ... Under a greatly extended program, the [latter] function would be greatly enlarged, but the existing general set-up of the NRC could administer such a system. ... A second alternative would be to ... administer research under a Department of Scientific and Industrial Research. ... There is no doubt that the present set-up of NRC is almost an ideal system, with its freedom from departmental regulations, and its right to hold property and receive funds from non-governmental bodies. But, on the other hand, I have often felt that, if and when research budgets rise to relatively significant figures, it is quite possible that more direct ministerial responsibility would be demanded by the government. ... Which system would work best in Canada over a period of years, I do not presume to say.

Yours sincerely

C.J. MACKENZIE

On December 13, 1943, Mr Howe replied, in part as follows:

Dear Dr Mackenzie:

I have your very interesting letter ... [and] wholly agree that the situation we are facing demands that scientific research in Canada be given a more prominent place.

I suggest that you should continue your study of a post-war organization for scientific research that will be in keeping with the magnitude of the task.

I intend to do all I can to see that research is given a prominent place in the government's post-war planning. In the meantime, your letter will help me to formulate my own thoughts on the subject.

Yours very truly

C.D. HOWE

Early in February 1944, while in Washington attending a meeting of the Combined Policy Committee (a tripartite committee of the US, UK, and Canada, on peace-time control of atomic energy), I had an informal conversation with Mr Howe. He told me that a few days previously the prime minister had informed his cabinet colleagues that, among other things, he was considering the setting up of a temporary Department of Reconstruction with Mr Howe as minister, and that he (Howe) had told the PM he did not want that portfolio, but, he added: 'I know that some day Mr King will summon me to his office and I will come out as minister of Reconstruction – so we had better start thinking about the role of science in that organization.'

On 2 October 1944, Mr Howe asked me to come around to his home that evening. He said he had formally agreed to take on the portfolio of Reconstruction and one of his conditions was that he become chairman of the Privy Council Committee on Scientific and Industrial Research. He said further that he was thinking of four or five divisions under directors general, who could act as a general staff and advisory board to the minister, and asked me if I would be willing to act temporarily as director general of the Division of Scientific Research and Development. He said he had already approached Dr W.A. McIntosh, Harry Carmichael, R.A.C. Henry, and Jack Berry, for he intended to be ready for action the day the department was officially set up. (Before the year end, divisional staffs had been recruited, and departmental regional officers were in operation six months before war ended in Europe.)

On 13 October 1944, I had received a message that the prime minister wanted to see me before one o'clock. This was the first time I had been in his private office and he was very gracious. He did not sit behind his desk; we sat on a lounge – he was very complimentary about the Research Council and myself; he said that General McNaughton was not returning to the National Research Council, and he would like me to accept the permanent presidency. We discussed many things and I stayed nearly forty-five minutes. There was very little discussion of the job; I told him what my conditions would be and he was quite agreeable.

In a radio broadcast that evening, the PM announced, among other things, Mr Howe's appointment as minister of Reconstruction and chairman of the Privy Council Committee on Scientific and Industrial Research. This would bring the Research Council into closer contact with the work of the Department of Reconstruction. The PM also said that research would be extended and more liberally supported in the post-war period.

For those of us interested in science, it was exciting news to hear, for the first time, from any prime minister of Canada, that research and development was to be extended and liberally supported in order to play a vital role in future government planning. It also meant that, with Mr Howe as chairman of the Privy Council Committee on Scientific and Industrial Research, the NRC could now revert to its normal peace-time procedures, which had had to be temporarily altered in wartime.

Since 1939 most of our projects had been 'top secret,' and only those persons actively involved could be cleared for access to pertinent classified documents and information. Instead of clearing top-secret matters through the minister of Trade and Commerce as chairman of the Privy Council Committee on Scientific and Industrial Research to whom NRC normally reports, we had had to channel such clearances through one of the several ministers of Defence or the minister of Munitions and Supply. This wartime improvisation would not have worked without the whole-hearted co-operation of the ministers of Trade and Commerce (the Honourable W.D. Euler from 1935 to 1940 and the Honourable J.A. MacKinnon from 1940 to 1948). As one with no previous experience in civil-service protocol, I am afraid I did not realize for some time the debt I owed these ministers, who made my activities so free of time-consuming and ineffective formalities, and who also honoured me with personal friendship and with wise advice I greatly valued.

Mr King's announcement that research would be extended and more liberally supported, moreover, gave a sense of reality to the long-term planning we already had begun at NRC. Our research directors began reorganizing their divisions accordingly, and implementation of plans was well under way by VE day.

Also, in this period, a real effort was made to strengthen NRC's contact with industry. As president, I made personal visits to most of the industrial research laboratories in Canada and our staff made contacts with their opposite numbers in their respective specialties in industry.

The wartime associations with our British and American friends continued, particularly in discussions of peace-time organization of science in view of its greatly increased size and impact on social and economic developments.

As victory became certain, the most important immediate task was to prepare specific estimates for the first post-war budget. After discussions with Mr Howe, I appeared before Treasury Board, outlined our long-term plans, and submitted the following recommendations for immediate action:

1. Continue the budget for NRC on the same scale of expenditure as in the last year of war, on the understanding that it would be doubled within five years as the necessary staff of competent scientists became available. (Since many predicted a post-war depression, and war expenditures were being drastically cut, this proposal in 1945 seemed quite bold.)

2. Give highest priority to the setting up of a military research organization to take over responsibilities for defence research policies.

3. Continue and expand our existing nuclear-energy programs for the peaceful uses of atomic energy.

4. Expand medical research.

5. Establish new research divisions of building research, radio and electrical engineering, applied chemistry, and applied physics, and laboratories in the Prairie and Maritime regions to serve the special needs of those areas of Canada.

The government accepted in principle all these policy proposals and provided budget items to cover the immediate expenditures involved. This acceptance of our plans and estimates in effect relieved NRC of its responsibility for military research policies and, by 1947, a Defence Research Board was formally established, with the approval of all concerned. Friendly co-operation between the board and the council existed from the start, and the board quickly established a reputation for successful service.

My term of office as president of the National Research Council (October 1944 to February 1952) covered active years of reorganization, extension, and consolidation, as the council changed back from war to peace. They were also turbulent years in the political arena.

During the demobilization period, there were fears that we might be entering a post-war economic recession similar to that experienced after World War I. Temporary war establishments were being liquidated, and key war personnel began returning to their pre-war positions. Except for financial commitments to social and welfare programs, including the re-establishment of returning veterans, retrenchment was the order of the day.

Inflation and labour unrest followed the lifting of wartime prices and wage controls and, from 1948 to 1950, threats of war in Korea and the Berlin crisis raised possibilities of our becoming involved again in military conflict. The Defence Research Board, set up in 1947, relieved NRC of its responsibilities for military research, but we continued to be prepared to operate our laboratories on research problems assigned to us by the military authorities, if and when a real emergency arose.

Mr Howe was under considerable unofficial pressure to re-establish a Department of Munitions and Supply, which he resisted; but eventually he did head a temporary Department of Defence Production. The war clouds cleared by 1951 but, while these threats existed, we on the council's administrative level became involved in studies concerned with civil defence and protection against nuclear attack, as well as tentative mobilization plans. Fortunately, these political crises did not reach far into our laboratories, except in certain special cases. In the main, our reconstruction programs and the day-by-day operations of our laboratory and extramural projects were not seriously disrupted.

Medical research had been organized by the late Sir Frederick Banting in 1938 as an associate committee of NRC on the understanding that, as soon as sufficient funds became available, it would become an independent council. Actually, from the start, direction had been exclusively in the hands of medical men who operated in an autonomous and efficient fashion. No sooner had the committee become well organized than war broke out. Characteristically, the medical scientists turned to war work with extraordinary speed and effectiveness; the associate committee remained a nucleus but, from 1940 to 1945, outstanding war contributions were made by three temporary associate committees on aviation, naval, and army medical research. With the end of the war, the temporary committees were disbanded and the main associate committee became, in reality, an NRC division (this division became the Medical Research Council in 1960) without laboratories of its own, but with rapidly expanding and well-directed programs of scholarships and grants in aid of research to workers in the medical schools across Canada.

The original Electrical Engineering Section in the Division of Physics, which had expanded so spectacularly in wartime in the radio and electronics field, became the Radio and Electrical Engineering Division, focused on adapting and extending to civilian use and industrial applications the techniques that had proved so successful in war. In a similar way, and for the same purposes, the applied section of the Chemistry Division became the Division of Applied Chemistry.

The original Division of Mechanical Engineering had, from the start in 1936, and particularly during the war, concentrated its major efforts on support of aeronautical research and the solution of urgent aviation problems in the services and industry. Military and civilian aviation have much in common and, during and after the war, increased demands for research into such interrelated fields as flight research, instrumentation, automatic controls, and safety continued to come from the Departments of Transport and Defence and the aviation industry. In 1959, the aeronautical section was reorganized into a National Aeronautical Establishment, administered by the council but in essence a co-operative project, serving the needs of several departments of government and industries in general. Apart from its aeronautical activities, the Division of

Mechanical Engineering built up important sections focused on research and applications in the sophisticated fields of mechanics, hydro-mechanics, and thermodynamics. It also developed special laboratories devoted to railway engineering, instrumentation, and low temperatures. All these operations render special and important service to the national and industrial needs of Canada.

At the Prairie Laboratory, founded in 1948, stress was placed originally on the industrial utilization of waste agricultural products and, at the Maritime Laboratory, founded in 1952, on the industrial applications of such products as seaweed. Regional laboratories, so set up, have the great advantage of being able to call on the extensive facilities of the central laboratories.

The new divisions just mentioned were really extensions of the type of research already being carried out in the Division of Applied Biology. The Building Research Division, founded in 1947, on the other hand, had a different origin and character and was set up to fill a gap in a mission-oriented field where applied scientific research was an urgent national need. This division was planned with wisdom and built up with unusual despatch by its first director, R.F. Legget. It was designed to function primarily as a co-operative scientific aid to the civil-engineering problems of the building industry in general, and as a research establishment in particular for the vital and comprehensive field of housing in all its varied aspects. Its laboratories were focused on urgent scientific studies in a field where, for much too long, outmoded empirical rules and procedures governed specifications and construction. Non-laboratory studies brought a National Building Code that introduced scientific rationality into a field where individual codes had often been based on local pre-judice and customs of yesteryear. Sections on standards for building materials were set up to reduce real costs. Architectural concern with design problems, such as space utilization, acoustics, and insulation, came to be studied jointly by interdisciplinary groups which did not consider factors of structural safety and economics incompatible with aesthetic values and reasonable amenities of living, so important to the comfort of a home owner. The division soon became an informal but very real scientific adviser to both the Department of Public Works and the Central Mortgage and Housing Corporation. In addition, committees of practising architects, builders, and experts from every field, interested in the details of planning and administration, became consultants and advisers to the division. In this way, the division achieved the unique result of bringing its contributions in applied science into direct contact with hundreds of professional designers and builders and thousands of individual consumers.

In 1954, when I had retired from responsibility as a public servant, I looked back at fifteen years in Ottawa, and wrote the following:

Certain things (not necessarily the most important) stand out in my recollections. I am still impressed by the ease with which the NRC changed to war work and back again to peace with a minimum of serious disruptions. Superficially, the variety and character of projects and the unorthodox ways with which they often had to be attacked seemed, to many, quite removed from pre-war activities. In reality, the fundamental responsibility of council, "to promote scientific and industrial research" for the benefit of Canada, is basically the same in war as in peace. One of the specific responsibilities, in the applied field, is to initiate and develop devices and systems. It also has the duty of transferring to appropriate establishments or to industry those projects which prove successful, and of liquidating those not viable. This has been done both in wartime and in days of peace: that the NRC has never been an empire builder is demonstrated by the histories of military, medical, and atomic-energy developments.

Physically, the 1954 NRC is very different from the institution that went to war fifteen years ago. Today there are eleven times more employees than in 1939 and the budget, due in part to inflation and modern sophisticated equipment, is also eleven times greater. The three basic research divisions remain the same in number but, on the applied side, instead of one applied-research division (as in 1939), there are now (including two regional laboratories) six applied-research laboratories and divisions and, as well, a Technical Information Service to assist small industries across Canada. It interests me that, over the years 1939 to 1954, while the growth of both pure and applied activities has been rapid, the expansion of the applied divisions has been much greater. However, the fundamental role of the council's laboratories has not changed. Conduct of so called mission-research programs is not its primary role, but there is a responsibility to initiate researches and developments that may eventually lead to large, independent, mission-oriented programs. Assisting industries in any way possible has always been an objective; such assistance takes on widely different forms depending on specific circumstances and demands. The council's assistance to REL during the war was very different to that given Polymer, and the association of NRC with the atomic-energy project was of a different order of magnitude.

The history of atomic-energy developments in Canada, from the first small laboratory experiments to the creation of a large, mission-oriented, industrial complex by 1953, affords a striking demonstration of the effectiveness of the council's flexible structure in adapting its services to particularly complex and changing needs. The first step taken, in late 1942, was the setting up of a small exploratory research laboratory in Montreal; this the council, by its constitution, could do, and did, without further reference. However, the final policy decision to build a multimillion-dollar plant at Chalk River was made by cabinet; construction and future operational contracts were between a private industrial company (Defence Industries Limited) and the minister of Munitions and Supply.[1] During the early wartime phase, selected groups of NRC specialists were in reality seconded to the project, and I acted informally as executive representative of Mr Howe throughout. The NRC as such, however, had no legal responsibilities for policy decisions or funding, although many divisions and sections gave much voluntary advice and assistance.

In 1947, the government set up the Atomic Energy Control Board, with complete responsibility to cabinet for all matters in this still highly secret field. As construction of the first sizable reactor neared completion in 1946, the industrial company (DIL) indicated that it wished to cancel its management contract. AECB then requested the Research Council, as the only other Canadian group experienced enough, at that time, to take over the management contract from DIL. As the atomic-energy project rapidly expanded, particularly in its program for the development of nuclear power plants, it became obvious to all concerned that this was not a proper role for the NRC and that a separate Crown corporation should be set up for that purpose. This was done and the Atomic Energy Company of Canada Limited formally took over the staff and facilities at Chalk River on 12 February 1952. This ended the official association of NRC with the atomic-energy project.

World War II was often called "a physicist's war," because most of the spectacular innovations were based on physics and mathematics. The demand everywhere was for able physicists experienced in applied research. In 1939, in the NRC laboratories, a few physicists were working on war projects but outside this relatively small effort, little applied research in physics was being done anywhere in Canada. By 1943, however, we had in Canada sizable groups of scientists and scientific engineers performing admirably in this field. How did this happen? When war was declared, distinguished university professors, graduate students, and research physicists from all over Canada volunteered in large numbers and became applied researchers for the duration. The successful formation of mixed working groups of pure and applied scientists brought a combination of talents and experience that made the production of the whole greater than the sum of its parts; of more permanent importance, there was created the mutual respect between pure and applied researchers, so vital for modern national scientific achievements.

In 1914, the ideological gap between pure and applied science seemed as wide as that between Darwinian scientists and fundamental theologians. By the end of World War II, this was no longer the case. The line between pure and applied science had narrowed and, in many sophisticated projects, had almost reached the vanishing point: the ancient philosophy that pure and applied scientists should be separated and segregated in unilingual monasteries and industrial laboratories is no longer valid. Pure research, however, is ambivalent. It has a direct cultural role and is also the material base of technological advances. No modern country can be considered really civilized if it does not accept pure research as an essential part of its culture and, from a materialistic standpoint, no country can hope to take an effective part in meeting national emergencies or capitalizing on innovations, that does not consider pure research an essential overhead of its scientific technology. It was Faraday, for instance, a pure scientist, who first demonstrated the theory of electro-magnetic induction; but, before this idea could give birth to rich applied benefits, it took physicists like Lord Kelvin, knowledgeable enough to perceive the implications of such a currently abstruse idea, and with enough imagination and enterprise to envisage the practical possibilities for electrical power plants and transmission lines. Most modern revolutionary advances in technology, such as electronics and nuclear energy, have followed the same sequence: an original idea in the creative mind of an individual, followed by the practical exploitation of the idea by an army of applied scientists, engineers, entrepreneurs, industrialists, and statesmen.

A century ago, the time interval between the idea and economic exploration was measured in decades. The first atomic bomb was dropped seven years after fission was discovered; in the future, original ideas discovered Saturday afternoon will probably be discussed in industrial research laboratories on Monday morning. It is obvious that, to be prepared to meet national emergencies or to capitalize quickly on major technological innovations, a country must have strength in both pure and applied science, and the scientists in each category must have respect and sympathy for the work and interests of the other.

The strains of war emphasize both strengths and weaknesses. In the years after World War II, in the United States, scientific statesmen became acutely aware that their country's impressive strength in technology was, in great measure, the fruit of pure research carried on quietly in Europe and elsewhere over many years. They quickly realized that, since the time gap between idea and industrial utilization had been reduced dramatically in recent years, no country could in the future be strong industrially if its ratio of pure- and applied-research activities was out of balance; as a consequence, in the post-war years, plans were made for proportionately greater expenditure on pure research. In England, however, enlightened scientists became acutely aware that Britain's imbalance was the opposite; the findings of their own pure research, in all too many cases, had been the basis of most profitable applications in countries other than Great Britain. To correct this imbalance, Sir Henry Tizard and others advocated the setting up of institutions (like the MIT in Boston) where scientific engineers could be trained in an environment where pure and applied science are considered equal and essential components of a strong scientific technology. In Canada, the imbalance between expenditures on pure and industrial research has been even more pronounced and, in the reconstruction period, serious efforts are being made to build up the applied and industrial component. But, in both England and Canada, it has become evident that increasing the ratio of the industrial-research component is much more difficult, expensive, and time consuming than increasing substantially the less costly pure-research component in a country with a massive industrial competence.

As a participant in both World Wars, and the reconstruction periods that followed, the thing that now stands out most vividly, in my mind, is what happened in those post-war reconstruction years. Experiences in World War I impressed both Great Britain and the United States with the superiority of Germany in the fields of scientific improvisation and in industrial research. During the post-war years, the phenomenal growth of applied and industrial research led the United States to its preeminence, with which the world is familiar. Canada made no such effort to follow the example of her neighbour, but remained happy to take advantage of a prosperity based on a branch-factory industrial pattern that brought modern technological 'know-how' in certain fields, but little competence in industrial research or innovation: between the two wars, Canada remained essentially a scientific colony. True, a few Canadian scientists had joined wartime research establishments in World War I, but there was no organized participation by Canda as such. In fact governments, industries, and the general public showed little real interest in

scientific research and technology during the war, and the only government reaction came as the result of a formal suggestion from the
government of the United Kingdom that Canada should follow her
example and set up a Council for Scientific and Industrial Research in
Canada. With little public interest or enthusiasm, an act incorporating the
NRC was passed in 1916: however, the doors of the council's laboratories
were not opened until 1932, sixteen years later, but fortunately in time for
service in the next war.

Things were very different after World War II. In the six years of war,
Canadian science and technology, led by the initiative of NRC, had come of
age. By war's end, its standing was high amongst scientists in our allied
countries and, of most importance, was recognized at home. This in turn
brought unanimous and enthusiastic support from both governments
and the general public. As Prime Minister Mackenzie King announced on
13 October 1944, in his restrained manner, "Research will be extended
and more liberally supported in the post-war period."

In an address in 1954 I told a story about reconstruction days which,
although true, was not restrained. The following extracts, I think, reflect
the enthusiasm and atmosphere of the time:

'I go back to one of the real crises in World War I.

'This had to do with one of the many critical shortages in chemicals.
You will recall the ammunition shortage in Flanders in 1914 and 1915.
The demands for cordite could not be met. The situation was desperate.
One of the most urgently needed chemicals was acetone, the former
sources from hardwood and fusel oil being completely inadequate.

'In the frantic search for new sources, Lloyd George heard of the work
of a quiet, modest research professor of chemistry at Manchester who, in
his attempts to make butadiene, had found a fermentation method of
making butyl alcohol, but unfortunately, as the professor saw it, there was
also produced acetone in quantity.

'The professor's failure was great news for Lloyd George, who wanted
acetone above all things. He immediately got in touch with the professor.
Pilot-plant studies were initiated and soon plants were being built in the
United Kingdom and Canada and later in the United States; the most
successful at the time was that at the Gooderham Works in Toronto,
Canada. One crisis had been met and the war went on.

'That was great drama in 1916, and the fact that the professor, Chaim
Weizmann, thirty years later became the first president of Israel may not
be purely coincidental, but neither has it to do with my central theme this
afternoon.

'Incidentally, this story illuminates some fundamental truths about research; it illustrates the nature and unpredictability of fundamental research; that is, looking for one thing (butadiene), and finding the solution to a different and acute problem. It also emphasizes truths we have learned the hard way; that without fundamental, unfocused research there can be no accumulation of scientific capital; that without a trained corps of applied scientists within a country's boundaries to take advantage of fundamental research, there will be no national dividends; that without national understanding of how research really works, neither of these will be provided.

'But to get back to the main point of my story.

'At the end of World War I, what happened? In Canada operations ceased immediately and the doors of the acetone plant were closed. In the United States, similar plants were *not* dismantled but became the nucleus of a great industrial development in North America; the surplus butyl alcohol, together with war-surplus nitrocellulose, became the raw materials of the nitrocellulose lacquer industry based on solvents and cellulose, another component of cordite.

'What happened in the case of our acetone factories happened also in the case of our aircraft, chemical, and other war industries.

'The opportunities were there but Canada, the country to whom the twentieth century was to belong, was not scientifically ready in 1918.

'Now a flash to 1940, another war and another critical strategic shortage – rubber. Incidentally, one of the key components of artificial rubber was the same butadiene that Weizmann was looking for in 1914 when he discovered a new method of making acetone. It is also an interesting speculation that Weizmann might have developed artificial rubber twenty years before the Germans did had he not been diverted from his research.

'What did Canada do about this rubber shortage?

'Again in association with her allies, she built and put into operation with speed and efficiency a most intricate artificial-rubber plant based on scientific techniques that we formerly thought were practical only in research laboratories.

'The significant difference, however, is that, at the end of World War II this factory was *not* dismantled as was the acetone plant in 1918. The operation was kept going as a Crown corporation, Polymer Ltd, and today is one of the vital components of a young, rapidly growing, and vital chemical industry so essential to any country.

'I have used this story of our artificial-rubber factory not because of its special importance but to illustrate what happened in most of our war and other plants, and to indicate the significant changes that have taken place in the scientific approach and outlook of our engineers and industrialists.

'Now, how did this take place? What was the fundamental difference between the Canada of 1918 and that of 1945 which accounted for this change in procedure?

'In 1918 we had enterprising industrialists, reasonable skills, and no dearth of natural resources; we had a few research scientists in universities, and plenty of competent and resourceful designing, construction, and operating engineers, but we had few real applied scientists and development engineers, and there was no definite public recognition of the vital national need for co-ordinated, vigorous and native applied research. In 1918 we were still colonial-minded in the realm of applied science.

'In 1945, the situation was very different. By 1939 we had created a sizable corps of highly qualified and experienced research scientists and scientific engineers. We had strengthened immeasurably all our government establishments and our universities, and industry everywhere had become interested in the applications of science. We had the resources of men with experience and confidence to organize quickly extensive research and scientific services for our industries, without which no such operations can remain permanently successful.

'In addition, however, and of paramount importance, there had developed by 1945 a strong public conviction that Canada's economic future must rest on a strong and progressive Canadian science and technology.

'These changes in outlook and potential may seem to have appeared suddenly. In fact, the results apparent today are based upon the unspectacular work of twenty years during which our fundamental scientific forces and facilities were being slowly but soundly built up.'

Ten years of reconstruction, 1944 to 1954, has seen the universities of Canada attain international status, largely through the rapid increase of NRC grants in aid of research and for scholarships. The rate of increase in industrial research has been equally spectacular: in 1939 there were small control laboratories but only a few real research establishments. By 1954 over four hundred industrial companies had active research programs and their total expenditures on research had risen from a relatively insignificant figure to over one hundred million dollars per year.

This growth of science and scientific technology in the past decade has been impressive; the pace of acceleration extraordinary. However, acceleration cannot be maintained continuously; there will be periods of pause and even recessions. But the basic strength of Canadian science is now so strong that, as long as excellence and service remain the aim, recessions may retard but cannot destroy it.

Volumes have been written about Canadian-American relations and the problems involved. Statesmen and scholars have been concerned, in the main, with political, economic, and environmental matters; little thought has been given to what I believe is the central core of Canada's policy for scientific technology. Let me illustrate: few Canadians have yet realized how profoundly our scientific developments during the war were affected by the fact that the United States did not enter World War II until the attack on Pearl Harbor in December 1941. I have become convinced that, if America had declared war in September 1939 instead of twenty-eight months later, the status of Canadian science would have been far different from what it is today.

During those twenty-eight months, United States branch factories were barred from participating in the manufacture of the secret, sophisticated weaponry being developed in Britain, while we in Canada were privy to such secret plans. This meant that, for the first time in many years, we were on our own, built special factories, and were producing sophisticated equipment for several months, free from American competition. This demonstrated that, when free from the overpowering industrial resources and competitive marketing power of American industry, Canada's scientific and industrial engineers could and did produce such equipment as efficiently and as acceptably as those of any other country. It is difficult to escape the firm conviction that, if the NRC had not had a two-year head start on research and development of prototypes for war equipment, Canada would have come out of World War II with little more capability in current science and industrial technology than it did after World War I and, in all probability, the current high standards and prestige of our universities, research institutions, and industry would not have been achieved for several decades. This is why I believe a principal aim of our government's policy for science must be to protect the gains made in six years of war; how to maintain a viable science must now be considered one of Canada's Canadian-American problems.

Canada has many advantages; it is a middle-sized industrial country with abundant natural resources, a mature science and technology, and an enlightened citizenry. Our scientists, technologists, and industrialists have immediately available, from a friendly, generous, and powerful neighbour, probably the world's best source of up-to-date information and industrial know-how. Our friendly neighbour, however, is also superbly enterprising, competent, and competitive, lives very close to us, speaks our common language, but does not always understand our culture and way of life.

These circumstances affect our real autonomy in many ways, but particularly in the way our industrial complex has been shaped. It seems to me that the gut issue of broad national policy for science is political and economic, not scientific. Canada's future as an industrial country will not depend on the details of how scientists and engineers are organized and where they work in their laboratories and factories. It will, rather, depend on how well a few, at least, of our political leaders and senior public-service officials realize the importance of science and develop a real understanding of what science is all about, what the essential environmental conditions are for first-class scientific output, and how the authoritative voice of experienced science can best be presented – and really listened to – in the pre-decision deliberations of government.

[1]Mr Howe followed the US pattern of letting construction and operating contracts to private industry.

Selected Biographical Index

BALLARD, BRISTOW GUY Head of electrical engineering in the Division of Physics, NRC, from 1930 to 1946. Assistant director of the Division of Physics and Electrical Engineering, NRC, 1946. Director of Radio and Electrical Engineering Division, NRC, 1948. Vice-president (scientific) of the NRC, 1954. President of the NRC, 1963–67.

BANTING, FREDERICK GRANT Co-discoverer (with C.H. Best) of insulin, 1921. Winner of the Nobel Prize in Medicine (with J.J.R. Macleod) in 1933. Director, Banting and Best Department of Medical Research, Toronto, 1923–41. Captain and major in the Canadian Army Medical Corps, 1939–41. Adviser to the director general of Medical Services, 1940. Member of the War Technical and Scientific Development Committee, 1940. Member of the NRC, 1937–41. First chairman of the Associate Committee on Medical Research, 1938; chairman of the Associate Committee on Aviation Medical Research, 1940. Died 21 February 1941, in a crashed bomber on the coast of Newfoundland.

BELL, RALPH PICKARD Appointed a member of the Executive Committee of the Department of Munitions and Supply, and director general of aircraft production, in 1940. A member of the Canadian section of the Joint Defence Production Committee, 1941. Appointed aircraft controller, 1942.

BEST, CHARLES HERBERT Co-discoverer (with Sir Frederick Banting) of insulin, 1921. Research associate in the Banting and Best Department of Medical Research, Toronto, from 1923 to 1941. Initiated the Canadian Serum Project – the development of dried human serum for military use – in 1939. Became director of the Banting and Best Department of Medical Research in 1941, and was a surgeon captain in the RCN, as director of the RCN Medical Research Division, 1941–6. Member of the NRC, 1947–53.

BOYLE, ROBERT WILLIAM One of a small group of distinguished scientists who laid the foundations of research activities in the Royal Navy, with his war research in the Anti-submarine Division of the Admiralty Board of Inventions and Research, 1916–19. Director, Division of Physics and Electrical Engineering, NRC, 1929–49. Distinguished for his work on ultrasonics. His greatest contribution to Canada was in his selection of potential-leader staff for the NRC Division of Physics and Electrical Engineering, a long-continued process in which he seemed to be both inspired and infallible.

BRAGG, SIR LAWRENCE Winner of the Nobel Prize for Physics in 1915. Cavendish Professor of Physics at Cambridge, 1938–53. One of the high-ranking British scientists assigned to work as liaison officers to the NRC during the war.

BURTON, E.F. Wartime member of the NRC, when he was professor and head of the Department of Physics, and head of the McLennan Laboratory, at the University of Toronto.

CAMBRON, ADRIEN Joined the Division of Chemistry, NRC, as a research chemist in 1930. Became assistant director (1946) and co-director (1950) of the Division of Chemistry, and director of the Applied Chemistry Branch (1950).

CAMPBELL, WALLACE RONALD President, Ford Motor Company of Canada Limited, 1942; chairman of the board, 1946. Chairman of the War Supply Board. Member of the NRC, 1937–43.

CAMSELL, CHARLES Deputy minister of Mines and Resources, 1936–45. Member of the NRC, 1924–36. Member of the Territorial Council, Northwest Territories, 1921–35; commissioner, 1935–46.

COCKCROFT, SIR JOHN Fellow, St John's College, Cambridge, 1928–46; professor of Natural Philosophy, Cambridge, 1939–46. Chief superintendent, Air Defence Research and Development Establishment, Ministry of Supply (UK), 1941–4; member of the Tizard Mission, 1940; director of the Atomic Energy Division, NRC, 1944–6. Winner of the Nobel Prize for Physics, 1951.

COLLIP, JAMES BERTRAM Member of the NRC from 1938 to 1946, when he was professor of Biochemistry and director of the department, McGill University

(1928–41), and Gilman Professor of Endocrinology and director of the Research Institute, McGill (1941–7). Director of the Division of Medical Research, NRC, 1946–57.

COOK, WILLIAM HARRISON Joined the NRC as a research scientist in 1930. Director, Division of Biosciences, NRC, 1941–68. Executive director, NRC, 1967. Serves on federal, interdepartmental, and NRC committees concerned with agriculture, scientific research, and university-support programs. Chairman of the Standing Committee on Grants and Scholarships, NRC. Research interests range from applied work on refrigerated storage and transport of foods to basic biochemical studies on proteins and lipoproteins. Has published more than 150 scientific and technical papers.

DONALD, JAMES RICHARDSON (RITCHIE) Director general of chemicals and explosives in the Department of Munitions and Supply, 1939–45; director general of chemicals and explosives in the Department of Defence Production, 1951–2.

DUNCAN, JAMES STUART Career in Massey-Harris-Ferguson Company Limited, concluding as president and chairman of the Board, 1909–56. Acting deputy minister of National Defence for Air, 1940. Member of the NRC, 1943–49. Director, Atomic Energy of Canada Limited, 1957.

EAGLESON, STANLEY PRESTON Clerk of the NRC, 1917–22; secretary of the NRC, 1922–6; secretary-treasurer of the NRC, 1926-45; general secretary of the NRC, 1946–57.

EULER, THE HONOURABLE WILLIAM DAUM Federal minister of Trade and Commerce, 23 October 1935 to 8 May 1940.

FETHERSTONHAUGH, EDWARD PHILLIPS Dean of Engineering and Architecture, University of Manitoba, 1923–49. Director of the radio technicians' course for the RCAF, 1941. Member of the NRC, 1938–46.

FIELD, GEORGE SYDNEY Research physicist in the Division of Physics and Electrical Engineering, NRC, from 1930 to 1946. Head of the acoustics laboratory, 1934. In 1941, was in the UK investigating anti-submarine and anti-mining devices for the NRC and the RCN. During the war, directed research on underwater warfare and acoustical aspects of telecommunications systems for all three services. Naval Research adviser to the Defence Research Board, 1947. Deputy director general, DRB, 1948. Chief of Division "A," in charge of naval and telecommunications research, and scientific adviser to chief of the Naval Staff, 1952. Chief scientist to the DRB, 1954. Vice-chairman, DRB, 1964–6.

FLOOD, EDWARD ALISON Joined the Division of Chemistry, NRC, in 1935. In 1940 became a lieutenant-colonel in the Canadian Army; from 1941 to 1947, was in charge of Canada's chemical-warfare laboratories. Head of research on active absorbents, NRC, 1947.

FOWLER, SIR RALPH HOWARD Member of many committees concerned with the defence of the UK, 1939-44, and as such familiar with and active in nearly all secret British military research. During the war became a liaison officer to the NRC.

GARDINER, THE RIGHT HONOURABLE JAMES GARFIELD Federal minister of Agriculture, 28 October 1935 to 21 June 1957. Minister of National War Services, 12 July 1940 to 10 June 1941.

GRAHAM, DUNCAN ARCHIBALD Colonel in the Canadian Army Medical Corps, and consultant in medicine to the director general of Medical Services, Ottawa, 1940-2. Member of the NRC, 1941-7.

GRAY, J.A. Wartime member of the NRC, when he was Chown Science Research Professor, Queen's University, Kingston, Ontario.

HENDERSON, GEORGE HUGH Professor of Mathematics and Physics, King's College; professor of Physics, Dalhousie University; and physicist, Victoria General Hospital, Halifax; 1924-49. From 1943 to 1949, chief superintendent of HM Canadian Naval Research Establishment, and operational research adviser to the C-in-C, Canadian North West Atlantic. Member of the NRC, 1946-49.

HENDERSON, JOHN TASKER Chief of the Radio Section of the NRC, 1933. Officer in the RCAF, 1942-6. Scientific adviser to the Canadian delegation to the United Nations Commission on Atomic Energy, 1947. Head of the Electricity Section, Division of Applied Physics, NRC, 1949. First recipient of the McNaughton Medal (1969), awarded by the Institute of Electrical and Electronic Engineers.

HISCOCKS, RICHARD D. Joined the NRC in 1939 to work on structural engineering. Head of the structures laboratory, NRC, 1944-5; worked on development of a wind tunnel and aircraft design. Chief technical engineer, subsequently director of Research and Future Projects, de Havilland of Canada, 1945-69. Vice-president (scientific), NRC, for industrial-research assistance and promotion, 1969.

HOWE, THE RIGHT HONOURABLE CLARENCE DECATUR Federal minister of Railways and Canals and minister of Marine, 23 October 1935 to 1 November

1936. Minister of Transport, 2 November 1936 to 7 July 1940. Acting minister of Transport, 13 May 1942 to 5 October 1942. Minister of Munitions and Supply, 9 April 1940 to 31 December 1945. Minister of Reconstruction, 13 October 1944 to 31 December 1945. Minister of Reconstruction and Supply, 1 January 1946 to 14 November 1948. Minister of Trade and Commerce, 19 January 1948 to 21 June, 1957. Minister of Defence Production, 1 April 1951 to 21 June 1957.

HOWLETT, LESLIE ERNEST Joined the Division of Physics, NRC, in 1931. Chief scientific liaison officer for Canada in London, 1941–42. Assistant director of the Division of Physics, NRC, 1948; associate director, 1949; co-director, 1950. Director, Division of Applied Physics, NRC, 1955.

ILSLEY, THE RIGHT HONOURABLE JAMES LORIMER Federal minister of National Revenue, 23 October 1935 to 7 July 1940. Minister of Finance, 8 July 1940 to 9 December 1946. Minister of Justice, 10 December 1946 to 30 June 1948.

JOHNSTONE, JOHN HAMILTON LANE Professor of Physics at Dalhousie University, 1922–45. Principal research officer, NRC, 1940–3. Commander in the RCNVR, 1943–5. Director of Operational Research, RCN, 1943–6. Captain in the RCNVR, 1945–6. Head of the Department of Physics, Dalhousie, 1945–56; dean of Graduate Studies, 1949–56. Member of the NRC, 1949–56. Member of the board of governors of the Nova Scotia Research Foundation, 1949–56.

KEYS, DAVID ARNOLD Consulting physicist, US Bureau of Mines, 1929; geophysicist with the Geological Survey of Canada, 1929–30. Professor of Physics at McGill University, 1929–47. Member of the NRC, 1945–55. Vice-president (scientific), NRC, 1947–55. Scientific adviser to the president, Atomic Energy of Canada Limited, Chalk River, Ontario, 1955.

KLEIN, GEORGE JOHANN Joined the Division of Physics, NRC, in 1929. Designed new wind tunnel for the NRC. During the war, designed gun sights, fire-control instruments for the coast artillery, an automatic stabilizer for an anti-submarine weapon, the mechanical design of the low-energy atomic pile at Chalk River, tracks for over-snow military vehicles, and skiis for aircraft. Became one of the three top world experts on snow classification. Developed a special wheelchair drive for quadriplegics; an automatic suturing device for surgery on veins and arteries; and invented storable extensible antennae for spacecraft, used in the Gemini and Apollo programs.

KUHRING, MALCOLM SHERATON Joined the Division of Mechanical Engineering, NRC, in 1930 and set up the fuels and lubricants laboratory. In 1931, set up the engine laboratory and became head of that section. Initiated work on the icing of aircraft (1936) and began icing work on jet engines, which became a co-operative project with the UK (1946). Chairman, NRC committee on smoke-laying craft, 1943–44, and test pilot of an experimental hydrofoil craft which was the first to go into heavy seas, operating at 40 mph in ten-foot waves. Chairman, Associate Committee on Petroleum, NRC, 1951–53.

MAASS, OTTO Professor and chairman of the Department of Physical Chemistry, McGill University, 1923–55, regarded as 'the' father of chemistry in Canada. Member of the NRC, 1939–45, 1947–53. Principal research officer, NRC, 1955–58. Gave invaluable leadership in all chemical aspects of the war.

MACKINNON, THE HONOURABLE JAMES ANGUS Federal minister of Trade and Commerce, 9 May 1940 to 18 January 1948.

MASSEY, THE RIGHT HONOURABLE VINCENT High Commissioner for Canada in the UK, 1935–46. Chairman, Royal Commission on National Development in the Arts, Letters and Sciences, 1949–51. Governor General of Canada, 1952–9.

MCKINLEY, DONALD WILLIAM ROBERT Joined the Division of Physics, NRC, in 1938. During the war, supervised the development of long-range radar equipment. After the war, concentrated on radio studies of meteors, which have resulted in forty scientific papers and one book. Assistant director, Radio and Electrical Engineering Division, NRC, 1954; associate director, 1960; director, 1963. Vice-president (laboratories), NRC, 1968.

NEWTON, ROBERT Acting director of the Division of Biology and Agriculture, NRC, 1928–32; director, 1932–40. Dean of the Faculty of Agriculture at the University of Alberta, 1940–1. Member of the NRC, 1942–50. President of the University of Alberta, 1941–50. Director of the Research Council of Alberta, 1941–51.

PARKIN, JOHN HAMILTON Initiated aerodynamics research and teaching at the University of Toronto, where he designed and installed a four-foot wind tunnel in 1917. Assistant director of the Division of Physics, NRC, in charge of aeronautical research, 1929. Director of the Division of Mechanical Engineering, NRC, 1937–57; consultant to the division, 1957–62. From 1947 to 1957, was one of three members representing Canada on the Commonwealth Advisory Aeronautical Research Council. Was also one of three members representing Canada on the Advisory Group for Aeronautical Research and Development to NATO, 1952–7. Director, National Aeronautical Establishment, NRC, 1951–7.

PENFIELD, WILDER GRAVES Professor of Neurology and Neurosurgery at McGill University, 1928–56; neurosurgeon, Royal Victoria Hospital, Montreal, 1928–55; neurosurgeon, Montreal General Hospital, 1928–55; director of the Montreal Neurological Institute, 1934–55. Member of the NRC, 1947–53.

PIDGEON, LLOYD MONTGOMERY In 1937, took charge of magnesium research at the NRC. During his years with the council, invented and developed a method for extracting magnesium cheaply and efficiently, in practically unlimited quantities, from Canadian raw materials. In 1943, became head of the Department of Metallurgical Engineering at the University of Toronto.

RALSTON, THE HONOURABLE JAMES LAYTON Federal minister of Finance, 6 September 1939 to 4 July 1940. Minister of National Defence, 5 July 1940 to 1 November 1944.

ROGERS, THE HONOURABLE NORMAN MCLEOD Federal minister of Labour, 23 October 1935 to 18 September 1939. Minister of National Defence, 19 September 1939 to 10 June 1940.

ROSE, DONALD CHARLES Joined the Division of Physics, NRC, in 1930. Scientific adviser to the chief of the General Staff, 1943–5. Chief superintendent, Canadian Army Research and Development Establishment (CARDE), Valcartier, Quebec, 1945–7. Head of work on cosmic-ray physics at the NRC, 1947. Became associate director of the Division of Pure Physics at the NRC in 1961.

SCULLY, WILLIAM VINCENT THOMAS During the war, was commissioner of Customs; became a vice-president of the NRC in 1945. Federal deputy minister of Reconstruction and Supply, 1945–8. Deputy minister of National Revenue (Taxation), 1948–51.

SHENSTONE, ALLEN GOODRICH Special assistant to the president of the NRC, 1940–5. Chairman of the Department of Physics, Princeton University, 1949–60.

STEACIE, EDGAR WILLIAM RICHARD Director of the Division of Chemistry, NRC, 1939–52. Deputy director of the British-Canadian Atomic Energy Project, 1944–6. Vice-president (scientific), NRC, 1950–2. President of the NRC, 1952–62.

THOMSON, SIR GEORGE Member of the Aeronautical Research Committee (UK), 1937–41. Chairman of the first committee on atomic energy, 1940–1. Wartime liaison officer to the NRC. Winner of the Nobel Prize in 1937. Master of Corpus Christi, Cambridge, 1952–62. Distinguished for his work on applied aerodynamics, the atom, and wave mechanics.

TIZARD, SIR HENRY In 1934, became chairman of the UK Air Defence Committee, which established fully operational radar chains on the British coasts before the war. Head of the 'Tizard Mission,' 1940, which arranged for the UK and USA to trade scientific war secrets and operational experience while the latter was still a neutral country; on this mission he came first to Canada and recruited three Canadians (including C.J. Mackenzie) to accompany him to Washington. After their return to Canada, at a private dinner, the main items of scientific and technical information were exposed to a group of senior members of the Canadian Cabinet. This was the beginning of understanding on the part of Canadian cabinet ministers of the usefulness of civilian scientists in the war.

TUPPER, KENNETH FRANKLYN Worked in the divisions of Physics and Mechanical Engineering at the NRC from 1929 to 1944, concentrating on the design of wind tunnels and other aero research facilities, the operation of seaplanes and a ship-model testing basin, and the design and operation of hydraulic structures. Was a member of the Canadian team assisting jet-engine development through low-temperature testing. With the Atomic Energy Division of the NRC, as assistant director of Research and director of the Engineering Division, 1946–9. Was responsible for the operation of the NRX reactor and the production of radioactive isotopes. Vice-president (scientific), NRC, 1964; vice-president (administration), 1968.

TURNBULL, LIONEL GRAHAM Joined the Division of Physics and Electrical Engineering, NRC, in 1937. From 1950 to 1960, conducted experiments in gravity and metrology. Since 1961, has been with the Electricity Section of the council.

VACHON, ALEXANDRE Dean, Faculty of Science, Laval University, 1937–9. Rector of Laval and Superior General of the Seminary of Quebec, 1939–40. Archbishop of Ottawa, 1940–53. Vicar General of Quebec, 1939. Member of the NRC from 1932 to 1944. Appointed by His Holiness to the College of Assistants to the Papal Throne, and created a Roman count, 1947.

WALLACE, FREDERICK CAMPBELL Brigadier in the Royal Artillery, 1939–45. Military member of Sir Henry Tizard's scientific mission to Canada and the USA, 1940. Adviser on development of Army radar, Radio Section, NRC, 1940–5. Vice-president in charge of production, Research Enterprises Limited, Leaside, Ontario, 1942–6. Member of the Defence Research Board and the NRC, 1949–55.

WALLACE, ROBERT CHARLES Principal and vice-chancellor, Queen's University, Kingston, 1936–51. Member of the NRC, 1932–42, 1948–51. Canadian representative at the London Conference which created UNESCO, 1945. Director of the Arctic Institute of North America, 1951–55.

Index to the Letters

An asterisk before a name indicates a person included in the Selected biographical Index.

of GL sets outlined 118–19;
efficiency surprises Sir Frank Smith
119–20; production not so
satisfactory 123
Review Committee of NRC: meetings
12, 93; studies post-war activities
130
Riverdale, Lord 19
Robinson, Sir Robert 95
Rockefeller Foundation: travel grant,
to assist Canadian scientists to visit
the US 81
Rodney 81
*Rogers, Hon Norman McLeod 28, 29,
38
Roosevelt, F.D. 90, 128n
*Rose, Donald Charles 57, 62, 75, 80,
86, 88, 89, 97, 101, 102, 106, 110,
111, 117, 118, 127
Ross, Dr J.H. 95
Royal Aircraft Establishment (RAE) 55,
60
Royal Air Force (RAF) 49, 67
Royal Canadian Air Force (RCAF):
difficulty in getting field tests because of strain on equipment 17;
contacts with NRC 21, 35, 50, 66, 69,
79, 81, 89, 109, 115; in Canada, essentially a training operation 102;
Henderson goes on operational
research 111–12; CRDF being manufactured for 114; has well-
organized operational research
groups 127; impressed with NRC
medical work 131. See also Liaison,
High-velocity shells
Royal Canadian Navy (RCN): relations
with NRC 21, 25, 32, 33, 35, 40;
makes NRC its scientific research

station 62, 75; enthusiastic about
Burr's work 63; enthusiastic re RDF
supplied 79; and for work done at
NRC 80, 88, 102; Rose's work developing rapidly 86; involved in
high-velocity gun project 89; one
RDF set saves five million dollars 111;
CRDF being manufactured for 114;
has well-organized operational research groups 127; re smoke-laying
craft 131
Royal Canadian Navy Volunteer Reserve (RCNVR): relations with NRC
staff 25, 28
Royal Engineering and Signals Experimental Board (UK) 19, 33
Royal Navy (RN): use of Canadian
scientists 28, 29, 33; supplies service
officer to the Tizard mission 49; uses
Canadian RDF 79; liaison with NRC
improving 111. See also: Admiralty
Royal Society 34, 35, 36
Royal Society of Canada: Mackenzie
and McNaughton both made Fellows
at Large 82

Salaries: unattractiveness of British
salaries 28; threatened by a general
directive 34; difficulty in paying
subprofessional staff an adequate
salary 77; the pinch of frozen
salaries for senior scientists 85–6;
loss of employees because government salaries are too low 96; lack of
adequate financial protection for scientists exposed to war dangers 97,
125–6; ban on promotions, effects
of 96; Mackenzie persuades Treasury Board to raise salaries of shop

04